HITTIN' THE TRAIL: WISCONSIN

Day Hiking Trails of
Douglas
County

By Rob Bignell

Atiswinic Press · Ojai, Calif.

DAY HIKING TRAILS OF DOUGLAS COUNTY
A GUIDEBOOK IN THE
HITTIN' THE TRAIL: WISCONSIN SERIES

Copyright Rob Bignell, 2015

Atiswinic Press
Ojai, Calif. 93023
hikeswithtykes.com/hittinthetrail_home.html

ISBN 978-0-9961625-0-0

Cover design by Rob Bignell
Cover photo of Wisconsin Point Lighthouse
on Wisconsin Point Trail
All interior photos by Rob Bignell

Manufactured in the United States of America
First printing August 2015

For Kieran

"I'm going to some place/Where I've never been before."
– Canned Heat, "Going up the Country"

Table of Contents

Introduction

I magine a place where you can hike miles of shoreline along the world's largest freshwater lake or stand at the base of a 16-story waterfall, where you can retrace the steps of ancient portages or hike a scenic river popular with American presidents, where the beaches you traipse yield up bear tracks or the woods you cross take you past rare, delicious berries. The place is real: It's called Douglas County, Wisconsin.

Tucked in Wisconsin's northwest corner, most of Douglas County's population is concentrated in the city of Superior, leaving lots of open space for outdoor recreation.

Recent geological history largely accounts for the county's layout. Glaciers during the last ice age scoured the landscape of topsoil and left behind plenty of sand that once sat under meltwater as the earth warmed. Because of this, pioneer farmers were slow to settle the area during the 1800s. The glaciers did leave behind a massive freshwater lake and river system that made for an ideal harbor, though, giving rise to the cities of Superior and neighboring Duluth, Minn.; they often are referred to as the Twin Ports.

Two of those riverways – the Bois Brule and the St. Croix – offered key transportation routes linking the Great Lakes and the Mississippi River that Native Americans and later European traders took advantage of in pre-railroad days. Today, both of those riverways are almost entirely protected, offering a plethora of recreational activities from fishing and canoeing to camping and hiking.

Communities

With the exception of the city of Superior, Douglas County is sparsely populated, dotted by small villages and several four-corner towns.

Though sporting a population of just under 30,000, Superior is an international harbor on the largest of the Great Lakes. The city might have been far larger and even more important if not for a pre-Civil War economic downturn. Though the first log cabin here was erected in 1853, within four years the population had risen to 2500 as excitement rose over a Lake Superior to Pacific Coast railroad, but the Panic of 1857 dashed those plans for a quarter century. Today, a number of multi-county trails that used to be rail lines start (or terminate, depending on your perspective) in Superior. In addition, the city's municipal forest offers a number of wooded hiking trails.

The hamlets of Brule, Maple and Poplar sit in the county's northeast corner. Each village sports a population of around 600 people. Brule is the gateway to the Brule River State Forest, a kayaking, fishing and hiking destination.

In the southeast, visitors to Douglas County first come across the village of Gordon and then Solon Springs. Both towns have a population of about 600 and offer access to the St. Croix National Scenic Riverway and the St. Croix River's headwaters.

Attractions

Douglas County boasts a number of outdoor attractions perfect for day hikers: two state parks – Amnicon Falls State Park and Pattison State Park – both with waterfalls; long stretches of the St. Croix National Scenic Riverway; and the Brule River State Forest that spills into Lake Superior. All offer several scenic hikes. Many excellent routes, including those that meander along Lake Superior, also can be found in Superior and just across the state line in Duluth.

Four major hiking trails popular with backpackers ramble through Douglas County. Among the most famous of them is the North Country National Scenic Trail, which runs 4600 miles from New York state to North Dakota. The Gandy Dancer State Trail terminates 98 miles to the south in St. Croix Falls, Wis., and heads through Minnesota for about a third of its route. Another old railbed turned hiking-bicycle path, the Wild Rivers State Trail, ends 104 miles to the southeast near Rice Lake, Wis. The Tri-County Corridor Trail links Superior to Ashland, Wis. over the course of nearly 62 miles.

When to Visit

The best months to day hike Douglas County are May through September. Depending on the year, April and October also can be pleasant.

As with the rest of Wisconsin, summers are humid, especially July and August. Rain can occur during the afternoon even when the morning is sunny, so always check the weather forecast before heading out.

November through March usually is too cold for day hiking. Once snow falls, trails typically are used for cross-country skiing, snowmobiling or snowshoeing. Early spring often means muddy trails thanks to snowmelt and rainfall.

How to Get There

Several major highways offer access to Douglas County.

From Minneapolis-St. Paul area, take Interstate 35 north then cross into Wisconsin on either the Richard I. Bong Memorial Bridge (aka U.S. Hwy. 2) or the Interstate 535/U.S. Hwy. 53 bridge. From northern Minnesota, head east on either Hwy. 2 or Hwy. 53 to Duluth and enter Superior via the aforementioned bridges.

From western Wisconsin, take either Wis. Hwy. 35 or Hwy. 53 north; both enter southern Douglas County. From eastern Wisconsin and the Upper Peninsula, drive Hwy. 2 to the county's eastern side. From central and southern Wisconsin, take either Wis. Hwy. 13 or U.S. Hwy. 51 north then Hwy. 2 west to Poplar.

Maps

Maps showing hiking trails, campgrounds, parking lots and other facilities are available online at *hikeswithtykes. com/headintothecabin_trailmaps.html.*

Featured Trails

Douglas County's hiking trails generally are clustered in three areas. **Lake Superior Country** includes those in the city of Superior and others in the county's northwest corner. **Brule River Country** are those in or near the Brule River State Forest in the county's northeast section. **St. Croix River Country** generally run along the St. Croix River in a swatch across the county's southern lands. Much of the southeast and central section of the county, despite being heavily forested, lacks public trails.

Lake Superior Country

D ouglas County's northwest corner includes a diverse array of trails, from hikes to the tallest waterfall in the state to walks along sandy beaches. The majority of the trails can be found within the City of Superior or at Pattison and Amnicon Falls state parks. Three of the routes – the Gandy Dancer, the Wild Rivers, and the Tri-County Corridor trails, are former rail lines turned hiking paths that head to other counties. Featured trails on this section are presented from north to south across the county and then from west to east.

Wisconsin Point Trail
City of Superior

Day hikers can walk part of the world's largest freshwater sandbar on the Wisconsin Point Trail.

The hike is a flat 3-mile one-way ramble down the center of Wisconsin Point along Lake Superior. Great times to walk the point include summer for the sunrises and either May or September for spotting migratory birds.

To reach the trailhead, from U.S. Hwys. 2/53 in Superior, turn north onto Moccasin Mike Road at Bear Creek Park. Next, go left/north onto Wisconsin Point Road, which curves onto the sandbar. Park at the first lot on the peninsula. The trailhead is at the lot's northwest corner.

Head northwest on the trail, which parallels the park road then drifts a little away from it. A sand beach stretches for 2.75 miles along the trail's right/northeast side.

Wisconsin Point and Minnesota Point, at 10 miles in length, combine to form the world's largest sandbar on a freshwater lake. The smaller of the two peninsulas, Wisconsin Point still is 203 acres in size.

Despite Wisconsin Point's narrow width, three major eco-systems converge on it. Much of the trail heads through stands of old growth pine and beach dunes. The trail also skirts marsh open water habitats, a favorite of migratory birds.

Near the end of the route is an Indian burial ground, a former cemetery dating to the 1600s for the Fond du Lac Band of the Ojibwe people. In 1919, the remains were re-buried at St. Francis Cemetery in Superior. Stone markers – and gifts ranging from walking sticks to teddy bears left by many visitors – can be found in the burial grounds.

At the trail's end is a scenic outlook with picnic table. From here, hikers can watch ocean-going vessels enter Superior Bay from Lake Superior. Minnesota Point is across the channel.

Northeast of the outlook is Wisconsin Point Lighthouse, sometimes referred to as the Superior Entry Lighthouse. The beacon sits on a pier sticking out from the point. You can hike to the lighthouse but not go into it; to reach it, you'll have to cross breakwater rocks that can be slick, so the walk is not recommended during bad weather or if with children.

There's no need to hike the entire 6-mile round trip trail. You can shorten the walk by parking at one of three other lots farther up Wisconsin Point Road.

Neither glass beverage containers nor horseback riding is allowed on Wisconsin Point. No fee or pass are required either.

• *Also see:* **Park Point Nature Trail** in St. Louis County

Osaugie Trail
City of Superior
Urban day hikers can learn about the heyday of Great Lakes shipping on the Osaugie Trail.

The 5.2 miles one-way trail passes several landmarks on the city of Superior's waterfront. Most day hikers will find enough to do on the now paved, former rail line that they'll need to break the walk into segments done on a couple of different days.

Begin the expedition by parking at the Richard I. Bong Veterans Historical Center. The center is at 305 E. Second St. near the U.S. Hwys. 2 and 53 intersection.

Upon parking, walk to the waterfront and look northwest to take in the view of Superior Bay. You may be lucky enough to spot one of the huge oceangoing ships that use the channel on their way to or from the city's docks.

Next, stop at the veterans historical center. It features several exhibits about Richard I. Bong, America's top World War II flying ace, and houses the actual Lockheed P38 Lightning he flew.

The trail southeast of the historical center parallels the channel separating the mainland from a sandspit. Looking northeast toward Lake Superior, the peninsula across the waterway is Minnesota.

Upon reaching Marina Drive, take a side trip by heading northeast to Barker's Island. There you'll find the *S.S. Meteor* Whaleback Ship Museum, a freighter built in Superior about 120 years ago. It was the last of a fleet of whalebacks that once lugged cargo to other inland ports on the Great Lakes.

Doubling back to the main trail, continue southeast. Barker Island is to your left. As you come to that island's southeast end, you'll spot rail lines on the left as well as piers. Following that is Hog Island.

The trail next crosses the Nemadji River, which is colored a deep, muddy brown. Large amounts of red clay wash into the river from upstream, giving the Nemadji its hue.

Past the river are the world's three largest ore docks. The longest one runs 2244 feet and stands 80 feet high; it can hold 100,000 long tons of ore, enough to fill 1435 train cars. It is from these docks that the famous *S.S. Edmund Fitzgerald* set out on its last voyage in November 1975.

Beyond the docks, the trail enters a residential area. It then crosses Bluff and Bear creeks, both of which flow into Allouez Bay.

On the bay's far side is scenic Wisconsin Point, a sandbar with miles of beaches. The Superior Entry Lighthouse sits on the sandbar directly northeast of Bluff Creek; this is the point in which ships using the city's docks enter and leave.

The trail ends at Moccasin Mike Road.

A multipurpose trail, the Osaugie also can be used for bicycling and in-line skating. It is handicap accessible.

Wild Rivers State Trail

Day hikers can enjoy a quiet stroll in the country on a former Wisconsin railbed turned multipurpose trail.

The 104-mile Wild Rivers State Trail stretches across three counties between Superior and Rice Lake. A fairly wooded 1.33-miles round trip section of the former C&NW Rail route runs at the trail's northern terminus, southeast of Superior.

Start the hike at the trail's intersection with County Road A, south of County Road Z and just north of County Road C. From the small parking lot at the trailhead, head southeast onto the gravel path.

The route quickly enters a forested area and angles away from the highway for a peaceful walk. Along the way, it crosses Brandt Road, so be sure to look both ways.

A good spot to turn back is at the Valley Brook Road intersection. You can continue onward, but while trees line the trail, you'll in quick order enter farmland.

Some of this segment can be swampy, so hike it in late

summer or autumn when water levels and bug populations are low.

A couple of other segments of the trail in Douglas County also make for good day hikes.

Farther down the line, start at Swamp Road for a 5.4-mile out-and-back hike across the Amnicon River and two other waterways to Mikrot Road.

In Solon Springs, the path runs through the village on its way between the Amnicon River and Gordon. To avoid highway noise, take the roughly four-mile route heading north from the municipal airport to County Road L.

On weekends, anticipate a variety of other users. Mountain bikers, horseback riders and ATVers also frequent the trail. In winter, you'll share the route with snowmobilers, cross country skiers and snowshoers.

Most of the trail surface consists of highway-grade compacted gravel and railroad ballast. ATV use has beat up the trail in some sections, but the entire stretch is traversable by foot with some segments at the southern end good for mountain bikes.

Also see Other Sawyer County Trails for descriptions of the route through nearby Minong and Trego.

Millennium Trail
Superior Municipal Forest

Day hikers can enjoy a leisurely stroll through one of Wisconsin's few remaining patches of boreal forests on the Millennium Trail in Superior.

The 1.6-mile trail sits in the Superior Municipal Forest, the third largest forest within a city in the United States. The Millennium runs from Billings Drive to Elmira Avenue on the city's southwest side.

A 10-foot-wide paved path, the trail sees minimal elevation change, staying about 630-660 feet above sea level. Because of this, it's a good trail for those new to day hiking or those who want to get into shape for a longer hike. Joggers, bicyclists and inline skaters frequently can be seen on the route.

To reach the trailhead, at the 28th Street and Wyoming Avenue intersection turn south to the municipal parking lot. The trail goes both east and west; skip the eastern side, which leads to multiple railroad tracks in Superior's industrial section.

Heading west from the lot, the trail runs through a wooded section of the municipal forest. Most of the trees here will be aspen, balsam, black spruce, cedar, white and red pine, and white birch. This is typical of a boreal forest, a northern woodlands dominated by coniferous trees.

Among the fauna are whitetail deer, which you likely will see along the way. During spring and summer, songbirds provide background music to your footfalls.

At about a quarter mile from the trailhead, the Millennium reaches a meadow and swerves south with woods on the east side and the open area on the west. In about 600 feet, the trail heads into the thicker wooded section of the forest, which often forms a canopy over the pavement.

The trail curves west about a little more than a mile from the trailhead then meanders the rest of its course through the boreal forest.

If you're a teacher or youth group leader interested in providing nature lessons, the Millennium marks a great trail to day hike. In addition to being an easy hike for kids, an outdoor classroom is located just off the trail, less than a mile from the trailhead. Six interpretive signs tell about the forest's history and ecology.

Upon reaching Billings Drive, return to the parking lot. The route runs 2.8-miles round trip.

Tri-County Corridor Trail

A pleasant woodland walk that includes a bridge over a rapids-filled river awaits day hikers on a segment of the Tri-County Corridor Trail.

The former Burlington Northern Railroad railbed turned hiking trail connects Superior to Ashland, covering 61.8 miles. As much of the trail parallels busy U.S. Hwy. 2, it's not the quietest of routes. An exception is a 1.2-miles round trip segment that skirts the southern edge of Amnicon Falls State Park from its west to east borders.

To reach that trailhead, take U.S. Hwy. 2 east from Superior. Turn left/north onto County Road U then take the very first left/west into Charlie's Riverside. Park on Charlie's backside; a connector to the main trail runs north from the lot. Upon reaching the main trail, go left/west.

The trail is mostly wooded with a good mix of evergreens and birch dominating.

The trail's highlight is the old railroad bridge crossing the Amnicon River, which flows north through Amnicon Falls State Park on its way to Lake Superior. The river's rocky shores and bottom make for a number of small rapids. The trail later crosses a creek that feeds the river.

As walking, keep an eye out for whitetail deer, fox, porcupine and other small mammals. Since the woodlands that the trail heads through joins the state park, there's a vast area for wildlife to flourish.

The trail opened in 1987. As a former railbed, the trail is wide with a surface of crushed limestone.

Kellogg Road marks a good spot to turn back.

The trail is open to horse riding and bicycling as well as ATVs. Be aware that it sometimes is referred to on brochures and websites as the Tri-County Recreational Corridor.

A couple of other segments of the trail also make noteworthy day hikes:

• **Superior** – Pick up the trail at 57th Avenue where the Osaugie Trail meets it and turn around at the second stream crossing for a 2.3-mile round trip.

• **Poplar** – The trail heads through town. To get away from the highway noise, try the roughly 2.25-mile one-way segment between Midway Road and County Road F.

• *Also see:* **Wentzel Lake segment** in Bayfield County

Amnicon Falls island trails
Amnicon Falls State Park

Hikers can view the results of an earthquake from 500 million years ago while walking the island trails at Amnicon Falls State Park.

Known as the Douglas Fault, this split in the earth stretches from Ashland to near the Twin Cities. Much of the bedrock sits at 50-60 degree angles, offering sights reminiscent of those along California's San Andreas Fault. All of these millennia later, the fault line still effects the course of rivers – which is to hikers' visual advantage.

To reach the state park, take U.S. Hwy. 2 east from Superior. Turn left, or north, onto County Road U. The park entry is in 0.3 miles. Amnicon Falls State Park is open each day of the year from 6 a.m. to 11 p.m. A vehicle admission sticker is required to enter.

Continue past the contact station across the bridge over the river and park in the first lot to the right; if it's full, continue on, taking the first road to right for another lot. Presuming you got a parking space in the first lot, pick up the trail at the picnic shelter and go right toward the Amnicon River. Listen for the sound of gurgling water, present the moment you open your vehicle's doors.

Because of the river's high mineral content, the waterway

sometimes can appear the color of root beer; it's clean, though, and swimming is allowed in designated areas. The river ultimately meanders north, flowing into Lake Superior.

The trail follows the Amnicon for about a quarter mile past another parking area and shelter (if you parked in the second lot, this is where you pick up the trail). Cross the river over a footbridge, which deposits you on an island where the waterway splits into two channels.

Go left for a view of Snake Pit Falls. While not particularly wide, the falls is 25 feet high with the water channeled between two stone works.

Continuing on, the trail loops around the island, offering a view of where the river divides. You also can garner a view of Lower Amnicon Falls. It tumbles over sandstone laid here more than 400 million years ago when streams flowed into a warm tropical ocean that covered Wisconsin.

The trail from there crosses the river via the 55-foot long Horton covered bridge, one of the park's major attractions. Originally a highway bridge at another spot on the Amnicon, it was moved here in 1930. It is one of only five Horton bridges that still exist. Besides experiencing history, hikers crossing the bridge are afforded two picturesque views – you can see waterfalls from both sides.

After crossing the bridge off the island, go left for a different view of Lower Amnicon Falls. Erosion has smoothed out the sandstone cliff here.

You might be pleasantly surprised by the amount of wildlife at the park. Black bear, coyote, fox, porcupine, raccoon, squirrels and white-tailed deer abound. Beaver, mink and otter – or at least their tracks – often can be spotted along the shore. A number of birds, including ruffed grouse and songbirds, also can be seen.

Backtrack and at the bridge continue straight, walking along the river banks for a view of Upper Amnicon Falls. The river rumbles over dark basalt, or solidified lava that formed here a billion years ago.

If you've noticed a number of gray, sparkling boulders, that's non-native rock. The stone is just tens of millions of years old; glaciers brought this granite gneiss here from Canada during the last ice age. Potholes in the rock also are fairly recent; swift-moving waters from melting glaciers drilled them out only a few thousand years ago.

Return to the bridge and cross back to the island. Go left for an island view of Upper Amnicon Falls.

Finally, cross the first bridge you took to reach the island. Follow along the same the path that you originally took to the island, maybe pausing for a picnic or snack. Past the second water source, the trail splits; go right to get back to your vehicle.

Thimbleberry Nature Trail
Amnicon Falls State Park

Thick with a variety of trees and wildlife, the Wisconsin Northwoods awes anyone who spends their weekdays working and living in a concrete jungle.

A good way to sample the Northwoods is the 0.8-mile Thimbleberry Nature Trail at Amnicon State Park. The trail includes a side trip to a pond that at one time was a brownstone quarry.

Upon entering the state park, continue past the contact station across the bridge over the river and pull into the third vehicle lot. It'll be the only one on the left and is located where the park road begins its loop around the campground.

The trailhead is to the north, across the road from the lot. Be sure to pick up, at the trailhead, an eight-page booklet that discusses plants found along the way, as well how Native Americans used them. The booklet's entries correspond to nine numbered signposts found along the trail.

The walking path quickly arrives at a trail junction. Take the trail straight toward the Amnicon River.

For most of the walk, the trail is wooded and somewhat hilly. Evergreens, birch and black ash are common here.

This first third of the trail parallels the river and offers several great views of it. You'll also find easy access to the river bed, which runs fairly flat about a fifth of a mile upstream from a set of three waterfalls. During spring, rushing water swirls through here and sometimes will rise above its banks.

Not quite halfway through loop, a spur trail leads to the sandstone quarry pond. From the late 1860s to 1910, the brownstone rock found all across the Bayfield Peninsula proved a popular building material, as it held up better than other stone during fires. Fifteen quarries, including this one, can be found in the area. The brownstone – formed when sediment settled and was buried some 500 million years ago – gave way during the early 20th century to concrete, which was cheaper, and bricks, which were more colorful.

If a hot day, the quarry pond is a great stop for kids, as they can wade into the water.

Upon returning to the main trail, go right/north. The trail gradually loops back to the stem trail you came in on.

Keep an eye out for the trail's namesake. Thimbleberries are a shrub whose five-point leaves look vaguely like a maple leaf. Their range is limited to the northern counties of Wisconsin and ranges into Michigan's Upper Peninsula. They prefer the sunlight of forest openings or edges, but older bushes will persist when the growing leaf cover finally shades them. Their fruit is edible, but people tend to have very extreme taste reactions to them, either loving or strongly disliking them.

Another interesting plant to watch for is Indian pipe. A white translucent color, it's a saprophyte, a class of rare plants that aren't green. Surrounding the Indian pipe's matted root fibers root system is a fungus that breaks down organic matter; the roots then absorb the nutrients. They can be found in the shaded understory of oak-pine forests, usually rising out of ground covered in pine needles.

A variety of animals also can be found here. Watch for deer and coyote tracks along the trail. Be aware that during dry years, wasps and hornets can become pesky.

Upon reaching the stem trail, go right/south, cross the road, and return to the parking lot.

Saunders State Trail

A pleasant stroll through the country awaits hikers on a segment of the Saunders State Trail in northwest Wisconsin.

The Saunders State Trail runs more than 8 miles long but need not be hiked in its entirety to be enjoyed. A 4.2-miles round trip segment between the unincorporated towns of Borea and Boylston works well for day hiking.

To reach this segment's trailhead, from Superior take Wis. Hwy. 35 south. Go west on County Road C. In Borea, turn right/north onto Irondale Road. After crossing the railroad tracks, you'll come to the trail. Park off the side of the road, and go west on the trail, as if heading back to Superior.

A former Soo Line railbed, the trail is flat and wide. The first section of the trail heads past farmland, but just enough trees line the route to offer a sense of walking down a wooded country lane.

In late summer, wild raspberries grow alongside the trail. A number of wildflowers also can be spotted from spring through summer.

At 2.1 miles, the trail reaches the gravel Mertes Road. This marks a good spot to turn back.

If you've got the energy, continue another 0.7 miles to Boylston where the trail curves north and then another 1.4 miles to its terminus just beyond Boylston Junction. Between these two communities, the trail borders a county forest.

Alternately, rather than head east from the trailhead, you can walk up to 5.7 miles west to the trail's terminus in Minnesota. Along the way, the trail crosses first the Pokegama River and then Clear Creek. The 3.3-mile segment from County Road W north of Dewey to the bridge at Clear Creek is particularly scenic and includes a bridge over the Pokegama.

Multiple uses for trail, including off-road vehicles, mountain bicyclists, and horses, are allowed.

Gandy Dancer State Trail

A rustic walk on a former rail line awaits day hikers on the Gandy Dancer State Trail.

The Gandy Dancer heads roughly north-south for 98 miles with a number of accessible points in Wisconsin and Minnesota cabin country, making it ideal for a day hike. It runs from St. Croix Falls, Wis., and enters Minnesota via a picturesque crossing of the St. Croix River in Danbury. It then re-enters Wisconsin in Douglas County south of Superior. The northernmost 15 miles of the trail (if including a connector with the Saunders State Trail) runs through Douglas County.

In Douglas County and Minnesota, the route sometimes is referred to as the North Gandy Dancer Trail, and for good reason. The northern section possesses a distinct sense of remoteness that the southern section, which passes through farmland and several small towns, sometimes lacks.

Still, access to the trail in Douglas County is plentiful. A

1.7-miles round trip section of the trail makes for a great day hike, taking walkers to the northern terminus.

To reach this segment's trailhead, drive Wis. Hwy. 35 south from Superior. At Interfalls Lake, turn right/east onto County Road B. Shortly after Point of Rocks Road, the trail crosses the rural highway. Park well off the side of County Road B.

Take the trail north. Though in farm country, a thick band of trees lines the wide path's western side. Fields are visible through tree breaks on the eastern side.

About 0.4 miles into the walk, the Gandy Dancer passes a long, narrow pond on its east side. The route shortly thereafter enters a small woodlands.

Built atop an old Minneapolis, St. Paul and Sault Ste. Marie railroad grade, the trail is named for the Gandy Tool Company workers who built the route back in the 1880s. Grade changes always are gradual, a necessity to accommodate the heavy trains.

As the pond gives out, the trail exits the woods and reaches a working rail line. This marks the northern terminus of the Gandy Dancer. Turn back here and retrace your steps back to your vehicle.

If interested in day hiking a more remote section of the trail in Douglas County, to the south a pleasant 2.85-mile stretch runs from South Foxboro-Chaffey Road over Balsam Creek to Drolson Road.

Big Manitou Falls overlook trails
Pattison State Park

Just a few miles south of Superior flows the highest waterfall in the Upper Midwest. Short overlook trails in Pattison State Park provide a variety of scenic views of Big Manitou Falls.

Summer marks the most comfortable time to visit the falls, but each season delivers a unique experience. Winter offers mist rising off the falls, spring brings thundering water flows, and autumn reveals the fantastic ancient rocks forming the gorge below.

To reach the park, take Wis. Hwy. 35 south about 13 miles from Superior. The entrance and parking lot is on the left.

For the trailhead, head to the southwest corner of the parking lot and take the pathway through the park's grassy picnic area past the nature center toward Interfalls Lake. Even though trees block the waterfalls, you'll be able to hear its rumble.

At the lake, follow the pedestrian tunnel under Hwy. 35. The half-mile-long trail's difficulty level is easy.

Past the tunnel, stay on the north side of Black River, which the Ojibwa Indians who once lived here called "Muc-udewa Sebee," translating to "dark." It aptly describes the brown-tinted river, the coloration caused by decaying leaves and roots spilling into the waterway.

Short trails leading off the main one give you two views of Big Manitou Falls. At 165 feet, the falls is the fourth largest east of the Rockies and the same height as Niagara.

The falls exists because of the dark basalt, the remains of a 1.2-billion-year-old lava flow that covers much of the Wisconsin-Minnesota border area. The Douglas Fault runs downstream from the falls, with the southern side of the fault rising at a 50 degree angle. Today, Black River runs down this gorge formed long ago by volcanic action and earthquakes, eventually meeting the Nemadji River, which flows into Lake Superior.

A century ago, developers almost wiped out the falls with a planned hydroelectric dam. The park's namesake, Martin Pattison, purchased land to deliberately block the dam's construction, however.

For a longer walk and additional views of the falls, head back toward the tunnel but before reaching it take a connecting trail that heads across the river. This provides two additional views of the falls from the south.

Though you'll probably be focused on the falls, keep an eye out for the local wildlife in this boreal forest. More than 200 bird species, including hawks and owls, as well 50-plus mammals, such as porcupines and black bears, call the park home.

On the way back to your vehicle, stop at the Gitche Gumee Nature Center for its exhibits. The popular state park also hosts nature programs and boasts a sandy beach. For children, the nature center loans out two different nature exploration backpacks full of fun activities. Pets on a leash are allowed.

Also, this is a carry in/carry out park, so you'll have trouble finding garbage cans.

Beaver Slide Nature Trail
Pattison State Park

A pleasant walk alongside a northern lake and a rapids-filled river awaits day hikers on the Beaver Slide Nature Trail.

The 2-mile trail in Pattison State Park often is overshadowed by its sister trails that lead to impressive waterfalls. But this is a peaceful walk worth making the time for.

To reach the trailhead, from Pattison's main parking lot head toward the 300-foot sand beach and follow it south along Interfalls Lake.

This is an easy route for families with children. Almost all of the trail consists of packed gravel and dirt and averages about 3 to 5 feet wide. The exception is a section running along a marsh, in which boardwalks make up the surface.

Seasonal creekbeds flow into the river, so there also are several small wooden bridges along the way. But while there are plenty of dips and rises, the trail avoids any hills.

The best views of Interfalls Lake are on the segment of the trail heading south from the beach. About 23 acres in size with a maximum depth of 13 feet, Interfalls Lake is home to largemouth bass, northern pike, panfish and trout.

Next, the trail intersects the Logging Camp Trail. Continue straight/right as the Beaver Slide begins to parallel the Black River.

The river in this stretch is about 30 feet wide and offers a number of rapids that provide a backing track of rushing water. Cedar, spruce, and a variety of pines hug the river's rocky banks.

As the trail reaches its southern end, you'll take a bridge over the Black River. Once across, go right/west; the Little Manitou Falls Hiking Trail heads the other direction.

The trail next rambles roughly northwest along the other side of Black River through a boreal northern forest, which primarily consists of evergreens. Large patches of ferns also can be spotted along the trail.

The trail then comes back to shoreline of Interfalls Lake. Upon reaching the lake's northwest corner, you'll arrive at a small dam that backs up Black River into Interfalls Lake. Continue curving around lake to the beach and your parking lot.

Before driving off, you might consider stopping at the Gitche Gumee Nature Center. It features a few exhibits about the park's wildlife, geology and cultural history.

Little Manitou Falls Hiking Trail
Pattison State Park

Day hikers can enjoy one of Wisconsin's highest waterfalls

on the Little Manitou Falls Hiking Trail in Pattison State Park.

The 2.2-mile round trip trail heads to the smaller of the state park's two waterfalls. Only part of the hike described here is the Little Manitou Falls Hiking Trail, as the Beaver Slide Trail must be taken to arrive at the trailhead.

To reach the trailhead, from Superior, head south on Wis. Hwy. 35. Pass the park's main entrance and take the next road on the left/east. Park in the lot and take the well-signed walking paths to the falls.

In 0.6 miles from the bridge, the trail reaches Little Manitou Falls. Wisconsin's eighth highest waterfall at 31 feet, the Black River rushes in twin torrents over basalt. Known among the Ojibwe Indians who preceded the pioneers as *Cacabeeca Bunghee* (or Little Waterfalls), this falls is less than a fifth the height of Big Manitou Falls downstream.

For those in your party who may not be able to handle the hike, a parking lot with picnic tables and toilets can be found near the waterfall at the trail's south end. This lot can be reached via Hwy. 35 south of the park's main entrance.

Other Lake Superior Country Trails

• **Snowshoe Trail** – Northern Wisconsin gets plenty of snow, dramatically changing the appearance of the landscape. During winter, Amnicon Falls State Park opens the 1.5-mile looping trail that takes visitors through a woods as well as above and out of the river valley. As the trail's name suggests, you will need snowshoes to cross it.

• **Pokegama Trail** – Located in Superior Municipal Forest, this 6.14-mile trail is popular with cyclists (A local cycling club actually maintains the trail.). The trailhead is north of Central Avenue east of the Cemetery Access Road intersection.

• *Also see:* **Bear Beach Trail**

Brule River Country

The famous Bois Brule River flows 44 miles through eastern Douglas County on its way to Lake Superior. Most of the river is protected by the Brule River State Forest. The 4600-mile multistate North Country National Scenic Trail also enters the county at the state forest. Featured trails on this section are presented from north to south across the county and then from west to east.

Bear Beach Trail
Bear Beach State Natural Area

A walk along a pristine sand beach awaits day hikers of the Lake Superior shoreline in the Bear Beach State Natural Area.

The unmarked trail runs for up to 3.4-miles round trip along narrow Bear Beach. While the Brule River State Forest begins with the wood line bordering the sand, the beach itself is set aside as a state natural area.

June through September mark the best time to hike the trail, but be sure to bring a sweatshirt or windbreaker. In addition, always check the weather and tide schedule; storm surges and high tide will inundate most of the beach with water.

To reach the trailhead, from Brule take U.S. Hwy. 2 west. In Maple, turn north onto County Road F. Next, go left/west onto Wis. Hwy. 13 then right/north onto Beck's Road. Park in the dirt lot at the end of Beck's Road near the Lake Superior shore.

From the lot, head northeast to the mouth of Pearson Creek. You'll need to wade the creek, which can reach about knee high, so always wear sandals and shorts, or be prepared to take off and put back on your hiking boots and socks.

Hiking the beach, you'll get a good sense of what this area of the world looked like before Euro-Americans settled it. A thick woods of paper birch, balsam fir, speckled alder, trembling aspen, white pine and white spruce hugs the beach's southern side while the lake stretches wide beyond to the north. Cobblestone and driftwood gardens also can be found.

Don't be surprised to see paw prints for bears in the sand and osprey flying overhead. Sometimes otters will play a game of hide and seek as they follow you from the safety of the lake's waters.

During migration season, the beach is a favorite of several bird species, especially gulls, shorebirds, snow buntings, terns and water pipits. They particularly congregate around the estuarine lagoons where the creeks flow into Lake Superior.

A number of small streams flow into Lake Superior, and as each needs to be waded, any one of them mark a good spot to turn back based on your energy levels. Haukkala Creek is a half-mile from the trailhead, and Nelson Creek is in 1.7 miles. Several smaller streams can be found between Pearson and Nelson creeks. You also can double the length of the hike by walking another three miles until the beach runs out near the Bois Brule River mouth.

Stoney Hill Nature Trail
Brule River State Forest

This short loop trail offers fantastic views of the scenic Brule River Valley.

The Stoney Hill Nature Trail runs 1.7-miles in the Brule River State Forest. If staying overnight at the Bois Brule Campground, the sunrise seen from atop Stoney Hill definitely is worth getting up for.

To reach the trailhead, from Brule, take U.S. Hwy. 2 west. Turn left/south onto Ranger Road, following it for a little more than a mile to the ranger station on the banks of the Bois Brule River.

Parking is available at the station.

From there, take the connector heading south to the nature trail.

As the river sits at about 950 feet elevation near the station, you'll have some climbing to do to reach the top of Stoney Hill. Parts of the trail will be steep.

One of the country's best cold-water trout streams, the Bois Brule also is a favorite of paddlers. Salmon can be found in the river, which meanders for 44 miles from wetlands near Upper St. Croix Lake to Lake Superior and drops 328 feet along the way.

The Bois Brule for many years was popular with outdoors-minded U.S. presidents. Privately-owned Cedar Island Lodge hosted five U.S. presidents – Ulysses Grant, Grover Cleveland, Calvin Coolidge, Herbert Hoover, and Dwight Eisenhower – with Coolidge spending the summer of 1928 there. Because of this, the Bois Brule has been nicknamed the "River of Presidents."

Interpretive signs along the nature trail describe the various trees found in the state forest. A variety of hardwoods, including oak, can be seen, and part of the trailheads through a pine plantation.

The top of Stoney Hill is at 1181 feet elevation and today hosts a radio tower and overlook. From the summit are good views of: the Bois Brule River with its Little Joe Rapids to the west and Doodlebug Rapids to the north; Hoodoo Lake to the south; and the Little Bois Brule River to the east.

Though pets are allowed in the state forest, they cannot be taken on this trail.

Brule River Outlet Trail
Brule River State Forest

Day hikers can wander among the remains of an ancient glacial lake that significantly shaped the Upper Midwest.

The Brule River Outlet Trail runs about 3-miles round trip in Brule River State Forest. An unnamed trail, it has been christened here for the major geological event that occurred in the region about 9000-8500 BC.

To reach the trailhead, from Brule, head west on U.S. Hwy 2. Turn left/west onto Afterhours Road. In about 2000 feet, as the road curves southwest, watch for unmarked trailheads on the left/southeast. Should the road curve straight west, you've gone too far. Park off the side of the road and take the trail southeast into the woodlands.

Upon hitting the trail, you're walking at the edge of ancient Glacial Lake Duluth near its outlet to the Bois Brule River. About 11,000 years ago during the last ice age, as the Superior Lobe glacier advanced westward over what is now the Wisconsin-Minnesota border area, it blocked the outlets of rivers flowing eastward. The water collected between the ice wall and the basin, resulting in several lakes.

When the lobe retreated, those lakes coalesced to form a larger one called Glacial Lake Duluth. Located in modern Lake Superior's southwestern corner, it stretched as far east as Marquette, Mich., and as far north as Grand Portage, Minn. It also covered what is now dry land in Wisconsin, Minnesota and Michigan, as the waterbody was 500 feet higher than modern Lake Superior.

After walking about 400 feet, the trail comes to its first major intersection; go right/west. The trail then zig zags for the next 1400 feet until cutting a straight line that heads southeast toward the Brule River.

In its day, Glacial Lake Duluth drained through the Bois-

Brule River south to the St. Croix River on its way to the Mississippi River. The hills to the trail's west – which reach 1100 feet elevation – marked the lake's shoreline. The trail itself would have been about a hundred feet below the lake's surface.

A major flashflood when an ice dam broke on Glacial Lake Duluth carved out the St. Croix River Valley to the southwest; many of the impressive geological features of Wisconsin and Minnesota Interstate Parks occurred during that flood. The lake also left a flat plain of red clay and sediment that sits on the modern Lake Superior shoreline of Wisconsin and Minnesota. Today, after a heavy rainfall, the mouths of rivers flowing into the lake can look red due to clay in the runoff.

After about 500 years, the glacial lake disappeared. As the Superior Lobe retreated, it left a gouge in the landscape that became Lake Superior and freed the local rivers' outlet to the other Great Lakes and the St. Lawrence River.

Since then, with the heavy glaciers' disappearance, the land has rebounded upward. The Bois Brule now flows northward into Lake Superior with the space between the Bois Brule and the St. Croix becoming a wetlands that sits at a higher elevation than either river.

Back on the trail, upon reaching the ridge overlooking the Brule, the route curves southwest and descends the bluffs to the river valley. In this area, the basin narrowed enough that the only place for the glacial lake to flow was an outlet into the Bois Brule about where modern Hoodoo Lake is.

The trail next reaches a jeep road just north of Little Joe Rapids. This marks a good spot to turn back.

North Country National Scenic Trail

Day hikers can walk several segments of what is considered one of the nation's premier long-distance trails.

Running 4600 miles from New York state to North Dakota, when completed the North Country National Scenic Trail will be twice the length of the Appalachian Trail and the longest hiking trail in the United States. Though the National Park Service studied the concept of a North Country Trail during the late 1960s, not until 1980 did Congress approve the route's creation.

New segments are added almost every year. At one time, the parking lot on County Road A in neighboring Bayfield County marked the trail's western terminus.

The trail enters Douglas County from neighboring Bayfield County at S. County Line Road, which is the Brule River State Forest's eastern boundary. In the forest, the trail follows high bluffs overlooking the Little Bois Brule River. A spur trail heads down the cliffside to the waterway just east of Winneboujou.

A peaceful segment to walk in the state forest is from Wis. Hwy. 27 (north of Radio Station Road) south to County Road S for a 6-mile round trip. Another option is taking the trail north for about two miles to Rush River Road from the same parking lot off of Hwy. 27; turn left onto Rush Road River, crossing Hwy. 27, for views of Big Lake.

Perhaps the best day hiking segments in the county can be found after the trail shifts south through the state forest and veers west, utilizing a famous historic portage connecting the Bois Brule River (which flows north into Lake Superior) to the St. Croix River (which flows south into the Mississippi River). This section is known as the Bois Brule-St. Croix River Historic Portage Trail. It then jogs north through a rare cedar bog ecosystem that can be crossed via almost 4000 feet of wooden planks on the Brule Bog Boardwalk Trail.

Next, the North Country heads through the town of Solon Springs. The trail generally is in good condition here with easy access from village streets.

Southwest of Solon Springs, the trail runs for six-miles through the Douglas County Wildlife Area, a managed pine barrens. At the St. Croix Flowage, it briefly enters the St. Croix National Scenic Riverway.

The trail then heads into some remote country as it crosses a long stretch of the Douglas County Forest. Much of this section is swampy or makes use of roads as it runs in a generally northwestern direction.

In Pattison State Park, the trail offers a double treat of first Little Manitou Falls then Big Manitou Falls, the latter of which is the Wisconsin's highest waterfall.

From the state park, the trail sticks to road routes as it exits Douglas County, entering Minnesota just south of Jay Cooke State Park.

For additional segments of the trail in Douglas County, also see Other St. Croix River Country Trails; in Bayfield County the **Erick Lake segment**; and Other Carlton County Trails.

Other Brule River Country Trails

• **Bayfield Road Trail** – The 2.25-mile loop trail in the Brule River State Forest passes through red oak stands that recently came under attack by two-lined chestnut borer, offering insights into the woodlands and a tree species man is trying to rescue. A connecting trail leads to the Copper Range Campground.

• **Brule River State Forest Annex trails** – North of Minong in Douglas County along County Road G lies a small area of planted forests along the Eau Claire River with multiple jeep trails running through them. From the end of the county road, hike west until the road curves north; take each of the three spur trails to the river for a 1.7-mile walk.

• *Also see:* **Brule Bog Boardwalk Trail**; **Brule-St. Croix River Historic Portage Trail**; and **Tri-County Corridor Trail** (Poplar)

St. Croix River Country

The St. Croix River begins its long journey to the Mississippi River in southeastern Douglas County, Much of the waterway is in the St. Croix National Scenic Riverway, but even the unprotected parts, which are exclusively in Douglas County, can be accessed and enjoyed by the public. Featured trails are listed south to north to the St. Croix River's headwaters.

Schoen/Louise Parks Jeep Trails
St. Croix National Scenic Riverway

Day hikers can ramble down a jeep trail heading from the bluff tops to the St. Croix River south of its headwaters.

During the river's first twenty or so miles downstream from the Saint Croix Flowage, there are few access points though all of it is located in the St. Croix National Scenic Riverway. Two exceptions are Louise Park and Schoen Park, located west of Gordon.

Schoen and Louise parks both offer a boat landing and spots to camp but not much in the way of hiking trails. However, between the two parks is a jeep trail that largely is in the national scenic riverway. It's a 0.6-mile out-and-back trail (1.2-miles round trip) that heads into the wilds of northern Wisconsin.

To reach the trailhead, from Gordon take U.S. Hwy 53 south and turn right/west onto County Road T. Regardless of the direction you came, turn south onto Rocky Branch Road. After the turn off for Louise Park, take the next left/south onto an unnamed road (If you've passed the access road to Schoen Park, you've gone too far south.).

Park off of the jeep trail near the intersection. The elevation is about 1045 feet above sea level.

From there, the trail gradually descends through a hardwood forest. In autumn, it offers an array of fall leaf colors, including brilliant reds and oranges to bright yellow and pine greens.

After 0.3 miles, though, the trail becomes steeper as it crosses an intermittent stream and then nears the river bottoms at about 940 feet elevation. Notice how the trees species change, with more pine and silver maples the lower you go.

As the trail reaches the river bottom, you'll hear the rush of water over its rocky surface. Boulders stick out of the shallow river in several spots along this stretch, especially about 400 feet upstream where they form a series of small rapids.

Return to the trailhead the way you came. There are no facilities on the trail.

Buckley Creek Barrens Trail
Buckley Creek Barrens State Natural Area

Day hikers can truly can get back to nature with a walk through a pine barrens near the northern reach of the St. Croix National Scenic Riverway.

The Buckley Creek Barrens Trail is an undesignated out-and-back footpath that runs 1.2-miles round trip through the Buckley Creek Barrens State Natural Area west of Gordon. Late summer and early autumn mark the best time to hike the trail, as spring through June will be wet and buggy.

To reach the trail, from U.S. Hwy. 53 in Gordon, head west on County Road Y. At about 4.4 miles, turn left/south onto South Lost Lake Road. After 4.3 miles, turn west onto Sunset Drive then in about a mile right/north onto Carp's Creek Road. The road runs north/south through the state natural area. In about 1.5 miles, you'll see a footpath on both sides of the road. Park on the shoulder here so other vehicles can pass.

Go east on the trail, which heads through Buckley Creek Barrens' higher elevations. The St. Croix River is a few miles to the east curving north.

In this region of Wisconsin, a number of wetlands and small lakes dot the landscape, surrounded by pine barrens – areas of sandy soil that support mainly pine and oak. The barrens once were the bottoms of a glacial lake that existed at the end of the last ice age, some 10,000 years ago.

The trail is a biologist's dream, especially for those studying the rare pine barrens ecosystem. After years of preventing wildfires – which flora in a barrens depends upon to maintain their life cycle – one broke out in 1997. A barrens much like that which existed before white settlers came to the area more than a century before has returned, providing a living lab.

Beyond jack pine and hill's oak, among the trees that you can spot on the trail are black and pin cherry. The wetlands host a number of grasses.

Because of this flora, butterflies and birds literally flock to the pine barrens. Among four rare Wisconsin butterfly species you might spot here are the cobweb skipper, the dusted skipper, Henry's elfin, and the Gorgone checkerspot. For birds, a number of thrashers, warblers and sparrows call the natural area home, and you might even spot an osprey or bald eagle overhead.

After 0.6 miles, the trail reaches a wetland's southeast tip. This marks a good spot to turn back.

State natural areas in Wisconsin typically don't have public facilities, and Buckley Creek Barrens is no exception. If you truly want to get into the wilds, this is a great hike. Be sure to wear insect repellent and wear pants and long sleeves when walking the trail.

On the drive back to Gordon along County Road Y, you'll

pass the St. Croix Flowage. This man-made lake often is mistaken for the St. Croix River's headwaters; it's also not officially part of the national riverway.

Brule Bog Boardwalk Trail
Brule River State Forest

Visitors to the Solon Springs area can day hike what feels like the forest primeval on the Brule Bog Boardwalk Trail.

Located in southern Douglas County's Brule River State Forest, the 2.3-mile boardwalk cuts through a wooded bog. Part of the North Country National Scenic Trail, it is entirely handicapped accessible.

To reach the trail, from downtown Solon Springs take County Road A north for about three miles, rounding the northern side of Upper St. Croix Lake. Watch for signs saying the North Country Trail is "1000 Feet Ahead" then turn into the boat landing where you can park.

Across the road from the parking lot, the trail heading right/northeast is the Bois Brule-St. Croix Historic Portage Trail. The boardwalk trail heads left or directly north.

An elevated boardwalk takes hikers through a conifer swamp at the bottom of a narrow valley. The valley marks a continental divide – all rivers to the south ultimately feed the Mississippi River while those to the north flow into Lake Superior, which is part of the St. Lawrence watershed.

In short order, the boardwalk crosses St. Croix Creek. You've now entered the heart of Brule Bog. Ferns and moss, as well as several varieties of orchids, cover the ground while white cedar, balsam fir, and spruce crowd out the sunlight.

Several rare plants and animals can be found in the bog. Among the insects you'll quickly notice is the zebra clubtail dragonfly. Songbirds include the black-backed woodpecker, golden-crowned kinglet, Lincoln's sparrow, olive-sided flycatcher, and saw-whet owl. Plants include the sheathed and the sparse-flowered sedge and the endangered Lap-land buttercup.

The sense of having traveled back in time to the ancient Carboniferous Period is temporarily interrupted as the trail crosses County Road P, which runs smack down the bog's middle.

After the county road, the boardwalk trail veers north-west. You'll come to the edge of the bog against a hillside, where the trail begins to meander. The uplands above the bog consist of sandy pine barrens.

Some 9,000 years ago as the last ice age ended, a river flowing out of the much higher Glacial Lake Duluth carved out the valley where the Bois Brule River, this bog, and Upper St. Croix Lake now exist. Released from the retreating glac-ier's weight, the land rose, causing water to flow in different directions and hence the divide.

The boardwalk ends at a spur off of Croshaw Road. This is the turnaround point.

A final note: You'll definitely want to apply insect repel-lant before hitting this trail.

Bois Brule-St. Croix River Historic Portage Trail
Brule River State Forest

Day hikers can walk what ranks among Wisconsin's oldest hiking trails – dating to 1680 but probably used as far back as prehistoric times – at the St. Croix River's headwaters.

The Bois Brule-St. Croix River Historic Portage Trail runs 4.4-miles round trip from Upper St. Croix Lake to the Brule River. It is part of the Brule River State Forest.

The trail can be a difficult hike through swampy territory so is best done by only adults or families with older teens. May through October mark the best time to hit the trail, but you'll need to bring bug spray for mosquitoes in spring and summer.

To reach the trailhead, from downtown Solon Springs, take County Road A north for about three miles, rounding the northern side of Upper St. Croix Lake. Watch for signs saying the North Country Trail is "1000 Feet Ahead" then turn into the boat landing where you can park. Across the road from the parking lot, take the trail heading right/northeast. The Brule Bog Boardwalk Trail heads left or directly north.

The historic portage trail is the same route crossed centuries ago by Daniel Greysolon Sieur duLhut (a French explorer who opened the way for fur traders in the 1680s), Pierre Lesueur (who established French stockades across this region in the 1690s), and Henry Schoolcraft (who found the source of the Mississippi River in the 1830s). Historical markers on moss-lined boulders along the trail tell their stories as well as other significant white explorers.

They selected this portage because it was a quick link between the Great Lakes and the Mississippi River. Upper St. Croix Lake is the St. Croix River's headwaters while the spring-generated Bois Brule River flows north into Lake Superior. It was the easiest way to traverse the Atlantic Ocean through the Great Lakes down the Mississippi River to the Gulf of Mexico...though for the marshy 2.2 miles between the Brule and Upper St. Croix, they would have to portage – or carry on foot – their boats and supplies.

As with so many of the early white explorers, Native Americans showed them the route. Local tribes had used the portage for millennia. Today, the Portage Trail is on the National Register of Historic Landmarks.

The portage was possible only because at the end of the last ice age some 10,000 years ago, a river flowed here from Glacial Lake Duluth, carving out a gorge and then the steep-sided valley. As the heavy glaciers retreated, the land rose in elevation, causing the river to dry up between the Brule and Upper St. Croix. The section that became the Brule reversed its course, as it now drops 420 feet over 44 miles from the portage to Lake Superior.

The trail is fairly narrow and at spots only shoulder-wide. It's heavily forested with leaves covering much of the path. Wild blueberries also grow along the trail.

There are some up and down climbs during the first mile as the trail parallels St. Croix Creek, which is on the left. Where the creek pools marks the St. Croix River's northern-most reach.

The out-and-back trail remains fairly flat to the Brule. After passing the Lesueur Stone, look on your left for the spring-fed creek that flows into the Brule. Upon reaching the river, turn back. The route is part of the North Country National Scenic Trail and continues north along the river.

Other St. Croix River Country Trails

• **North Country National Scenic Trail, Douglas County Forest segment** – South of Solon Springs, the seven-state North Country Trail crosses the Douglas County Forest for roughly three miles. It passes several idyllic ponds along the way.

• **North Country National Scenic Trail, Solon Springs segment** – The trail also cuts through the village. A pleasant two-mile route runs south of town to the county forest from South Holly Lucius Road/U.S. Hwy. 53 to Bird Sanctuary Road at the forest's edge.

• *Also see:* **Wild Rivers State Trail** (Solon Springs)

Neighboring Counties

Six counties surround Douglas County, each providing a variety of hiking trails that are easy to reach. The longest shared border is to the east with Bayfield County, where several walking paths, including the North Country National Scenic Trail, run through the Chequamegon National Forest. To the southeast, Douglas County has a tangental border with Sawyer County, which offers both the St. Croix National Scenic Riverway and the Birkebeiner Trail system. Washburn County, with the scenic riverway and Wild Rivers State Trail, is to the southeast. Burnett County, where the scenic river splits into its St. Croix and Namekagon sections, is to the southwest. Across the state line in Minnesota, Carlton County sits to the southwest and boasts the scenic Jay Cooke State Park. Most people coming to or from Douglas County do so via the bridges leading to St. Louis County in the northwest, where the city of Duluth offers a plethora of great hikes, including trailheads for the Superior Hiking Trail and the Willard Munger State Trail.

Bayfield County

A popular tourist destination, Bayfield County is the gateway to the Apostle Islands National Lakeshore. For those hiking Douglas County, especially in the Brule River area, a number of trails can be quickly reached in the Chequamegon National Forest. The North Country National Scenic Trail, as well as the Tri-County Corridor Trail, both continue east from Brule River State Forest into Bayfield County.

North Country National Scenic Trail, Erick Lake segment

The Erick Lake segment of the North Country National Scenic Trail heads along a ridgeline through a new growth forest.

About 61 miles of the North Country Trail crosses Bayfield County. The Erick Lake segment of it runs four miles one-way.

To reach the trail, from Iron River head south on County Road A. South of the second intersection with Bradfield Road, park in the lot on County Road A's southeast side. The North Country Trail heads both northwest and southeast from the lot. Go left/northwest from the lot and cross County Road A.

At 0.12 miles from the trailhead, the Erick Lake Segment gains elevation, climbing to one of the higher points along the trail, a hill at 1286 feet above sea level. From there, the dirt path follows a ridgeline as heading through woods and pine barrens.

At about 1.9 miles from the trailhead, the route crosses Banana Belt Road. From there, the trail generally descends as heading toward the segment's namesake.

In another 1.9 miles, Erick Lake comes into view on the

trail's north side. An 8-acre lake with a maximum depth of 26 feet, public campsites are nearby.

When the segment reaches Pero Road (aka Hughes Town Hall Road farther north), about 0.08 miles from the lake, turn around. The complete hike runs 8-miles round trip.

Drummond Woods Interpretive Trail
Chequamegon National Forest

Massive trees from an old growth forest and vibrant autumn colors await day hikers on the Drummond Woods Trail in the Chequamegon National Forest.

The 0.75-mile trail runs through the Drummond Woods, where a number of trees survived the 1800s logging of the Wisconsin Northwoods. The route sometimes is referred to on maps and in literature as the "Drummond Woods Trail."

To reach the trailhead, from Drummond, take U.S. Hwy. 63 north. In one mile, turn left/west onto Old 63 N (aka Forest Road 235). About 150 feet from that intersection on the right is a small pull-off for parking.

From the lot, take the stem trail northwest into the Drummond Woods. Coming to the loop, go left/west or clockwise. The loop is flat and fairly easy for children.

Heading through a northern hardwood forest, the trail marks an excellent spot to enjoy fall colors: the yellows of basswood and birch; the oranges of sugar maples; and the scarlet of black ash and red maple. Evergreens dominate the canopy with towering white and red pines and hemlocks.

The hemlocks are particularly impressive. Some of them measure 40 inches around.

The ground cover also offers a show, especially in spring. Violets, trillium and humble bellwort grow amid princess pine. When reaching wetter areas, blue flag iris flourishes in clumps.

A little more than halfway through the hike, the trail runs alongside a tamarack-black spruce swamp. On the ground, look for Labrador tea, leatherleaf, and pink lady slippers.

One other surprise is the carnivorous pitcher plant, which traps insects in its blossom and then digests them. Slippery petals cause bugs to fall into a liquid pit and drown.

Along the loop's north side, you can extend the hike by taking the intersecting North Country National Scenic Trail into the backcountry.

If visiting the region during winter, the trail is popular among snowshoers.

Other Bayfield County Trails

• **Anderson Grade Trail segment, Rainbow Lake Wilderness Area** – The 4-mile trail crosses the Rainbow Lake Wilderness Area from east to west over rolling terrain. Balsam fir, Northern hardwoods, paper birch and pines line the trail near Drummond.

• **Antler Trail** – Six trails make up the Drummond Ski Trail system southeast of town. This 2-mile route heads over gentle terrain through a Northern hardwood forest.

• **Flag River Walking Trail** – North of Iron River on Flag Road a half-mile from Battle Axe Road, the trail meanders west near the Flag River. Groves of Northern hardwoods and evergreens shade the path.

• **Iron River National Fish Hatchery Trail** – Three miles of trails cut through 1,200 acres of the U.S. Fish and Wildlife Service's Iron River National Fish Hatchery facility. A 2.4-mile segment running from the visitor center to the Weidenaar Road, combined with a stop at the hatchery, can make for a fun and educational day.

• **Long Lake Picnic Area Trail** – This 1.2-mile trail near Iron River in the Chequamegon National Forest circles Long

Lake and includes a boardwalk into a marsh. A picnic area is on the grounds; a parking fee is required.

• **Porcupine Lake Wilderness Trail** – Over a mix of rolling hills and fairly flat terrain, the Drummond area trail cuts through a forest of hemlock, maple, oak and white pine. Expect to see white-tailed deer, loons, and songbirds galore, as well as signs of bear, coyote and fox.

• **Rainbow Lake Wilderness Area trails** – Six miles of the trail crosses the Drummond wilderness area from northwest to southwest. Built on an old narrow gauge logging bed, it passes four lakes.

• **Ruth Lake Walking Trails** – On Ruth Lake Road, a half-mile from the County Road A intersection near Iron River, trails begin on both sides of the highway. Go west to skirt the wooded southern end of Lake Ruth in the Chequamegon National Forest.

• **Tomahawk Lake trails** – Off of Moore Road about 1.5 miles from the Island Lake Road intersection, walking paths run through wooded areas outside of Iron River. Trails begin on either side of the road.

• **Tri-County Corridor Trail, Wentzel Lake segment** – The trail connecting Superior and Ashland runs through Iron River. East of town, take the segment east from Topside Road east past Wentzel Lake and a pond to Forest Road 417 for a 3.8-mile one-way hike.

• **Two Lakes Campground Trail** – A 1.5-mile trail loops around Bass Lake near the campground in the national forest. Northern hardwoods and pines tower over the trail near Drummond.

• For more Bayfield County hikes, see this title's sister book, **Day Hiking Trails of Bayfield County**.

Sawyer County

Though the border between Douglas and Sawyer counties is a mere point on a map, those staying in the Solon Springs area easily can enjoy all this neighbor to the southeast offers. Among the highlights are the extensive Birkebeiner Trail system, which spills over into Bayfield County, and the Namekagon River section of the St. Croix National Scenic Riverway.

Birkie Ridge Trail

Though known primarily for the annual ski race held on it, Wisconsin's massive Birkebeiner Trail system also makes a great hiking route in summer.

With more than 66 miles of trails, all maintained by the nonprofit American Birkebeiner Ski Foundation, "The Birkie Trail," as its fans affectionately call it, offers multiple trailheads, loops and variations. One segment that's easy to locate and hike is the 2.9-mile round trip Birkie Ridge Trail.

A new trail in the system, Birkie Ridge opened in August 2013. The Birkie system runs between Hayward and Cable with this segment in Sawyer County just south of the Bayfield County line.

To reach a trailhead in Sawyer County, from Hayward take U.S Hwy. 63 north. After passing the Northern Lights Road junction, the trailhead with parking lot is on the left/east.

The trail heads south from the lot then quickly turns east. Built for cross-country skiing and bicycling races, Birkie Ridge is wide and boasts erosion mats beneath its surface.

All of Birkie Ridge sits in a classic Northern hardwoods forest of sugar maple, basswood, beech, white ash, and yellow birch, making for a colorful autumn walk. During the first 0.3 miles of the hike, hemlock and fir is more common in the tree mix. About 1.2 miles in, the trail reaches a loop. Go right/southeast on a route that meanders through the woods.

The entire Birkie trail system is a 40-plus year project in the making. The first cross-country ski race was held on it in 1973; today, it's the largest race of its kind in North America, attracting about 10,000 participants and 15,000 spectators.

At 1.9 miles, the loop reaches a stem trail that connects to the Birkie Trail, which leads to other routes in the system. Upon reaching the stem's end, turn back. The stem trail runs 0.15 miles.

Northwoods promoter Tony Wise is largely credited with starting the race and helping to popularize modern-day cross-country skiing. In 1972, he built cross-country trails at his Telemark Ski Area near Cable then started the Birkie race a year later.

Upon reaching the loop's eastern terminus, go right/northwest to add a little variety to the hike.

The Birkie trail system gets its name from Norway's Birkebeinerrennet cross-country event, which commemorates when skiers in 1206 AD smuggled the king's illegitimate son to safety during a civil war. The skiers were soldiers in the Birkebiener Party.

About two-thirds of a mile later, the loop reaches its western terminus. Go straight/west and retrace your steps back to the parking lot.

Be aware that the Birkie also is used by mountain bikers and joggers. There's plenty of space for both, but on race days the trail system will be closed to hikers.

Totagatic River State Wildlife Area Jeep Trail
Totagatic River State Wildlife Area

Day hikers can ramble alongside one of Wisconsin's few remaining wilderness streams on a jeep trail in the Totagatic

River State Wildlife Area.

Though not a designated trail, the old logging road runs about a mile (2-miles round trip) through a forested area along the Totagatic Flowage's northwest side. The flowage marks a wide swath of the meandering Totagatic River, which in 2009 became the Wisconsin's fifth stream to receive Wild River status.

To reach the trailhead, from Hayward take Wis. Hwy. 77 north/west. Turn left/north onto Wis. Hwy. 27. Park off the road on the west side of Hwy. 27 across from Dam Road. The jeep trail heads northwest from the parking area.

Most of the trail is under the cover of northern hardwoods, which makes for a scenic walk during autumn.

The Totagatic runs 70 miles through five counties. Its headwaters are in southern Bayfield County. Popular among canoeists, the cold and clear river flows into Totagatic Lake then to Nelson Lake and into the flowage. Hwy. 27 and the dam split Nelson Lake from the flowage.

Expect to spot a number of waterfowl along the hike. The bird-friendly flowage was constructed in the 1950s, and the 272-acre Totagatic River Wildlife Area has long been designated a state waterfowl restoration area. A mix of habitats – from hardwood forests and open water to swamps and upland grasslands – make up the wildlife area.

If you ask locals about the river or read printed materials on it, you're likely to run into some confusing appellations. Spellings and pronunciations of the river are about as murky as its name suggests – "Totagatic" is derived from the Ojibwe word "Totogan," which translates as "boggy river." Maps, plat books, tour guides variously spell the river's name as "Totagatic" and "Totogatic." Local pronunciations range from "Tuh-TO-ga-tec" and "To-TA-ga-tec" to "To-to-GAT-ic" and "To-BA-tec."

From the flowage, the river heads roughly west. North-west of Minong, it turns south and eventually flows into the Namekagon River.

Back in the wildlife area, the trail peters out at the edge of the flowage, a grasslands that the river runs through the center of. As an old logging road, expect parts of the trail to be overgrown, so don jeans and insect repellent for the hike.

Other Sawyer County Trails

• **Blue and Orange trails** – Combining Hayward Recre-ational Forest's Blue and Orange trails into a 1.6-mile walk takes you through a woods past a wetland and then a scenic lake where wildlife is abundant. Pets are allowed at the rec forest.

• **Kissick Swamp Wildlife Area North Trail** – Park at the Kissick Swamp Wildlife Area lot on the south side of West Chippnazie Lake Road, west of the intersection with Com-pany Lake Road. A trail winds for about a half-mile one-way (1-mile round trip) through woodlands on the wildlife area's north side.

• **Namekagon-Laccourt Oreilles Portage Trail** – The St. Croix National Scenic Riverway trail south of Hayward me-morializes a famous 18th century route where fur traders and explorers carried their canoes between rivers. An easy, 0.8-mile loop, the trail heads through a second growth forest of mixed hardwoods and pines.

• **Pacwawong Lake Trail** – Less a walking path than a jeep trail for boat ramp access to Pacwawong Lake in the scenic riverway, this 0.4-mile round trip is remote enough that there won't be much if any traffic. From Cable Sun-set/Totalatic Road, head south on Mossback Road, taking the first left/east; park in the gravel lot at the boat ramp and walk back to the road.

• **Timber Lawn Trail** – The 1.2-mile round trip southwest of Hayward runs through woods to an overlook of the Namekagon's north shore in the scenic riverway. From Old 24/Nursery Road (which parallels U.S. Hwy. 63), take Timber Lawn Road south until it becomes a jeep trail, where you can park. You can extend the trail by making a loop from the overlook via the jeep trail that heads north back to your vehicle.

• For more Sawyer County hikes, see this title's sister book, **Day Hiking Trails of Sawyer County**.

Washburn County

The only expressway linking Douglas County to the rest of Wisconsin runs from Superior through Washburn County, making this region's recreational opportunities easy to reach. Among the highlights are the Namekagon River section of the St. Croix National Scenic Riverway and the Wild Rivers State Trail.

Totagatic Ski Trail

Multiple ski loop trails in winter serve as great day hiking paths in summer for cabin-goers in the Minong area.

Of the four Totagatic Ski Trail loops, try Loop A. At two miles round trip, it's the shortest as well as the closest to the parking lot so is easy to locate.

To reach the trail system, head a little more than a mile north of Minong village on U.S. Hwy. 53. At the second, or northernmost, intersection with Lakeside Road, turn left/ east into the parking lot.

A jeep trail runs west from the parking lot for 0.25 miles. Most of the trail is mixed hardwoods, consisting of sugar and red maple and basswood. On other loops, trails head through groves of replanted trees.

At the first divide in trail, head straight (or left/ west) to do the route clockwise. You're now officially on Loop A.

The trails run through a border area between two eco-systems – the North Central Forest and the Northwest Sands regions. The major difference is the former's soil is only 5-10 feet above the bedrock while the latter can have a separation of several hundred feet. In part because of this, the North Central Forest is better able to hold hardwood trees such as maples whereas the Northwest Sands consists of pine and shrubland.

In 0.25 miles, the trail comes to a junction. Go right/north on a section of trail shared with Loop B.

The North Central Forest also covers a lot of territory in Wisconsin; it can be found in 19 counties and stretches into Michigan's Upper Peninsula. Often when thinking of the "Northwoods," an image of the North Central Forest is what comes to mind for most Wisconsinites and visitors to the state.

The next trail junction comes in about 0.1 miles; at it, go right/north. The trail you didn't take heads onto Loop B, which in turn connects with loops C and D.

These trails, however, don't go near their namesake river, which is to the north by a few miles. In any case, the Native Americans' name for the area that includes Minong village and these ski trails translates to "Pleasant Valley."

After about 0.25 miles, Loop A veers east and gradually curves south. In little more than 0.9 miles, you'll reach the access trail that leads to the parking lot; go left/east back to the lot.

Trego Nature Trail
St. Croix National Scenic Riverway

A pleasant walk through the woods along a wild river await hikers on the Trego Nature Trail in the St. Croix National Scenic Riverway.

The trail is best done during summer when the shaded walk keeps hikers cool. Early autumn is a good time for those who enjoy fall colors.

To reach the trail, take U.S. Hwy. 63 north of Trego village. About 1.3 miles from the visitor center and after crossing the bridge over the Namekagon River, take the first right. The parking lot is at the end of this entrance road.

Look for the trailhead on the parking lot's east side. The

trail is fairly well-maintained. Watch for some steep inclines and narrow sections on curves, however.

The trail parallels the Namekagon River through a woods of pine and deciduous trees, with views of the waterway. Benches typically sit in the viewspots.

Hikers are likely to see a variety of wildlife or at least signs of it. White-tailed deer, turtles, fox, muskrat, bobcats, squirrels, snowshoe hares, and great blue heron abound in the riverway. Watch for otters and their slides, muddy paths cleared in the river's bank in which they move from land to water.

You also might spot lake sturgeon, Wisconsin's largest fish, especially if the water is low. They like to lay motionless beneath overhanging trees. In fact, the river's name comes from the Ojibwe Indian words that loosely mean "place of the sturgeon." Most of the sturgeon, however, are downriver below the Trego Dam.

After the footbridge, the trail loops back upon itself. Hikers can return to the parking lot the same way they came in. The trail comes to about 2.8-miles round trip.

Dogs are allowed on the trail if leashed. For safety, don't climb the river banks, as they can be slick.

On the drive back home, stop at the Namekagon Visitor Center for displays about the riverway.

Other Washburn County Trails

• **Trego Lake Ski Touring Trails** – A pretty hike through a Northwoods forest awaits hikers on the Trego Lake trails in the St. Croix National Scenic Riverway. Up to 3.5 miles of trails are groomed here for cross country skiing in winter but can be day hiked the other seasons.

• **Wild Rivers State Trail, Minong segment** – The former rail line turned hiking trail heads through Minong on the way from Trego to Gordon. Starting at South Limits Road, head south on the trail to Lakeside Lake for a roughly four-mile round trip.

• **Wild Rivers State Trail, Trego segment** – A tranquil stroll through the woods with a bridge view of the Namekagon River awaits day hikers on a segment of the Wild Rivers State Trail in Trego. The hike runs a little under 2.2-miles round trip.

• For more Washburn County hikes, see this title's sister book, **Headin' to the Cabin: Day Hiking Trails of Northwest Wisconsin**.

Burnett County

While a long drive from Douglas County's populated areas, Burnett County offers several excellent clusters of hiking trails, including the world-famous Crex Meadows Wildlife Area, the lengthy Gandy Dancer Trail, and Governor Knowles State Forest. The quickest trails to reach from Douglas County, though, are the St. Croix National Scenic Riverway and Big Bear Lake Nature Trails.

Namekagon Delta Trail
St. Croix National Scenic Riverway and Big Island State Natural Area

Families can day hike to a scenic delta at the confluence of the St. Croix and Namekagon rivers on a trail in Wisconsin's Northwoods.

A number of unnamed and non-maintained trails run near the delta in the scenic riverway. For convenience sake, I've named this 2.7-mile out-and-back trail the Namekagon Delta Trail after its primary geographic feature.

Some of the area that the trail crosses, including the confluence itself, actually is part of the Big Island State Natural Area, but the boundaries with the scenic riverway are indistinguishable.

Like a wishbone, the scenic riverway splits in Burnett County. One fork – the St. Croix River – continues northward to its headwaters while the other fork – the Namekagon River – heads eastward.

To reach the trailhead, from Danbury, take Wis. Hwy. 35 north. Turn right/east onto the paved road named Springbrook Trail (If you've crossed the St. Croix River, you've just missed the turn.). Next, turn left/north onto Namekagon

Point Road. The road stops at a vista of the Namekagon and St. Croix's confluence, which sits about 94 feet below. Park off to the side of the road.

Take the jeep trail that heads to the left/northwest. It quickly descends about 90 feet to the river valley, heading through a woods to the confluence for a half-mile.

The Namekagon Delta includes a sandbar that doesn't quite cut the St. Croix's width in half, but it does narrow the flow by diminishing the latter's depth. Only a hundred feet or so south of the delta, the St. Croix widens to the same distance as it was north of the confluence.

Heading back up the cliffside to the vista site, take the fairly flat primitive trail running southwest along the bluff line. Its trailhead is along Namekagon Point Road just south of the vista.

The bluff line stretch of the trail runs for 0.85 miles one way, offering views of the confluence and then the St. Croix River in the tree breaks. The large island in the St. Croix's center is Big Island. Where the primitive trail reaches a jeep trail (listed on some maps as "Snowmobile Trail") marks a good turnaround point.

During spring into late summer, mosquito repellent is a necessity at the confluence.

Big Bear Lake Nature Trails

The Big Bear Lake Nature Trails offer three great day hiking opportunities.

All three trails are accessible from the same trailhead. The Grouse Walk Trail is the shortest at a half-mile.

To reach the trails, from Danbury take Wis. Hwy. 77 north/east for a little more than 10 miles. Turn right/south onto Bear Lake Road; in about 1.5 miles, turn left/east into a sand parking lot. If you've reached the intersection with Lake

26 Road, you've missed the lot.

From the trailhead at the parking lot, go straight (the middle route). Going left takes you to the Big Bear Springs Trail for a 0.75 mile loop, which is fairly similar to the Grouse Walk Trail.

You're now heading clockwise on Grouse Walk Trail through a largely open grassland and shrubland with scatter-ed pines, so you'll definitely need hat and sunscreen for the hike.

The nature trails are located in the rare Northwest Sands ecological landscape, which angles across this corner of Wis-consin from the St. Croix River to just short of the Lake Sup-erior. Farm crops can't readily grow here because all that sep-arates the surface from underlying bedrock is glacial drift – sand, gravel and silt left during the last ice age.

About midway through the Grouse Walk loop, an inter-secting trail takes you east to the Big Bear Meadows Trail. The trail is more wooded and runs for 0.875 miles.

After curving southwest, the Grouse Walk Loop skirts the shoreline of a small pond that during dry years often is just a shallow depression. The loamy nature of the soil typically means that moisture drains fast through it.

Despite that, a number of kettle lakes from melted chunks of the last ice age glacier exist across the region. Among them is nearby Big Bear Lake; though these nature trails are named for it, that lake actually is a good half-mile to the northeast.

Circling to Grouse Walk loop's south side, you'll head through a small grove. Pine, aspen, birch and oak dominate the few stands of trees in the Northwest Sands. Upon exiting the stand, you'll have returned to the parking lot.

The nature area's other two trails include:

• **Big Bear Meadows Trail** – Take the Grouse Walk Trail to the junction with the stem leading to the Big Bear

Meadows Trail's loop for a 0.875-mile walk. Much of the walk is through an open pine barrens with the center section of the loop more forested.

• **Big Bear Springs Trail** – From the Grouse Walk trailhead, take the left/north of the walking paths for a roughly 0.75-mile walk round trip. The trail's stem heads through a forested area while its loop portion crosses a classic Northwest Wisconsin pine barrens.

Other Burnett County Trails

• **Gandy Dancer State Trail, Danbury segment** – Day hikers can walk across an old railroad bridge over the St. Croix River at the scenic riverway and the St. Croix State Forest on the Wisconsin-Minnesota border. In Danbury, parking for trail access is next to the walking route north of Wis. Hwy. 77 between Wis. Hwy. 35 and North Glass Street; take the trail north for a 2-mile round trip.

• **Namekagon Barrens Wildlife Area trails** – Enjoy a walk down any of the gravel roads leading into these sand barrens for a hike into an Andy Griffith-like backwoods. Watch for sharp-tailed grouse and the upland sandpiper.

• For more Burnett County hikes, see this title's sister books, **Day Hiking Burnett County, Wisconsin** and **Day Hiking Crex Meadows Wildlife Area**.

Carlton County, Minn.

E asy to reach from Superior simply by crossing the U.S. Hwy. 2 bridge into Duluth then heading south on Interstate 35, Carlton County provides some top notch hiking clusters. Most notable among them is Jay Cooke State Park. A bit farther south and decidedly wilder is the Nemadji State Forest. The Willard Munger State Trail and Gandy Dancer State Trail also run through Carlton County.

East Ridge Trail
Jay Cooke State Park

Day hikers can cross a swinging bridge above a raging river running over nearly 2 billion-year old rock on the East Ridge Trail at Jay Cooke State Park.

The 1.5-mile round trip trail is one of about 50 miles of hiking paths through the park just southeast of Cloquet and Carlton. To reach the park, from Superior cross the U.S. Hwy. 2 bridge into Minnesota. Turn south onto Interstate 35 then take the exit for Minn. Hwy. 210, driving east through Carlton. The park is about five miles from the freeway. Turn right/south at the River Inn Visitor Center and use the lot nearest the river.

The trail leaves from the parking area's southeast end. This actually is a stem for the looping East Ridge Trail, which is on the river's south side. The stem heads through a picnic area before reaching the St. Louis River.

A new $1.1 million swinging bridge opened in November 2013. To the delight of most kids (and adults), the 219-foot pedestrian bridge bounces and sways. It replaces the 1953 bridge damaged during 2012's floods.

Beneath the bridge is the raging St. Louis River, which rushes over exposed bedrock formed about 1.9 billion years ago when a vast sea covered this area of North America. Over the eons as the mud and sand compacted into shale and grey-wacke, heat and pressure converted the buried stone into slate. Then, about 1.1 billion years ago, molten rock worked its way through fissures and covered much of the ground, leaving black basalt in its wake.

Once across the bridge, go left/east. You're now officially on the East Ridge Trail, with this segment paralleling the river's edge. Raging floodwater from melting glaciers some 10,000 years ago formed the river's current course.

At Junction 29, go right/southeast. The rest of the trail heads through a hardwood forest whose green in summer rivals that of Oz's Emerald City. The leaves turn an impress-ive array of yellows, reds and oranges as autumn sets in.

Upon reaching Junction 30, go right. The trail meanders about quite a lot along this segment but essentially heads west. Watch for a number of animals as walking through the woods. White-tailed deer will be easy to spot, but also look for signs of black bear, timber wolf and coyote.

At Junction 31, head right/north. The trail at this point has looped back toward the river.

More than 180 species of bird make their home in the park, so keep an eye to the sky when the trail opens up. Among the most fascinating birds in the park are the great blue heron, the marsh hawk, and the pileated woodpecker.

Upon reaching Junction 28, go right. The trail is now in its homestretch. At Junction 32, turn left and walk along the river shore; the trail soon arrives at the swinging bridge. Cross and follow the stem trail back to the parking lot.

Christmas Tree Trail
Nemadji State Forest

Day hikers can enjoy a peaceful walk through a fragrant

evergreen forest on the National Christmas Tree Trail in Nemadji State Forest.

The three-mile (2.6 miles for loop plus 0.4-miles round trip for stem) trail sits in the northwest corner of the massive forest. In 1977, a white spruce cut from the Nemadji served as the National Christmas Tree in the nation's capital. Forestry officials created the trail in 1987, naming it in honor of that tree.

To reach the trailhead, from Minn. Hwy. 23 north of Nickerson, take County Road 146 south. The county road angles east; when it veers northeast, continue going straight, turning right onto Net Lake Forest Road. The forest road heads though a wetlands. After crossing Net Lake River, turn left onto the State Forest B 41 Road heading to Gafvert Campground and Day-Use Area. When that road forks, go right. Parking is available at the day-use area for Pickerel Lake.

The trailhead goes north from the looping road at the day-use area, near the restrooms. You'll start on the stem of a lollipop trail. The stem heads through a dense red pine forest with tallgrass underbrush.

For thousands of years before loggers and pioneers arrived during the late 1800s, the red pines along the trail were much larger in circumference. The red pines now are young, growing on what once were farms, since abandoned because of the poor sandy soil.

Upon reaching the loop, go left/clockwise. Birch lines the trail's left side while dark pines rule on the right. About 0.75 miles into the trail, it enters a more open area.

During spring and summer, listen for the black-and-white warbler, which likes brush and deciduous woodlands. Its song sounds like a squeaky wheel.

Other wildlife to watch for include white-tailed deer, raccoons, eagles and porcupine. The last usually can be spotted in treetops wherever you see fallen bark.

At about 1.05 miles, the trail crosses a bridge of split logs over a creek that feeds Cranberry Lake. This is a low wetland area common to the northern part of the Nemadji.

The forest is named for the Nemadji River, which in turn comes from the Indian word meaning "left hand." It's so named because the river is on the left side of Lake Superior's St. Louis Bay.

At 1.25 miles, on the loop's northeast side, you can take a spur trail 0.2 miles to a picnic area overlooking the Net River. An old beaver dam is located here. You'll see what this part of Minnesota looked like before settlement – red pines so large that you can't wrap arms around most of them.

Returning to the main loop, in about 0.5 miles you'll come to the National Christmas Tree Site, where the 1977 tree was cut. Five white spruces were planted to replace it, and a sign commemorating the tree is located there.

From that waymark, the loop heads back to the lollipop trail's stem, which you can use to return to your vehicle.

Other Carlton County Trails

• **Carlton Trail** – About 4.3-miles round trip, the Carlton runs along the St. Louis River's south side between trail Junction 27 and 28 in Jay Cooke State Park. Park at the lot for the swinging bridge and upon crossing it, turn right/west at trail Junction 32 then continue straight at Junction 28.

• **Gandy Dancer Trail, Hay Creek segment** – Hikers can walk the edge of a pine barrens and some forested areas on this 4-mile round trip trail in the massive Nemadji State Forest. Take Minn. Hwy. 31 north from Kingsdale; there's a parking lot at the state forest line. Follow the trail north, paralleling Hay Creek to the right. Go two miles to Moose Junction Trail and turn back at the junction.

• **High Trail** – This often overlooked 3.75-mile round trip out-and-back trail in Jay Cooke State Park sits close to the

Wisconsin border on the St. Louis River's south side. Park off the road on Minn. Hwy. 23 about a mile from the border. The trail climbs up in elevation to a lookout over the river.

• **Matthew Lourey State Trail** – From north of Nickerson, take County Road 146 to County Road 145 then Harlis Road/County Road 363; south of Bley Road, as the road turns east, look for parking lot. Follow the trail to the Northeast Extension Forest Road for 0.9 miles; turn back there for a 1.8-mile round trip through a largely wooded area that opens onto scenic meadows.

• **Mountain Goat Forest Road** – A small segment of the Fond du Lac State Forest sits between Jay Cook State Park and the Wisconsin border. The jeep trail runs about 3.6-miles round trip up and down a hill. From Minn. Hwy. 23, go south on Mountain Goat Forest Road (sometimes labeled on maps as Bandle Road) into the forest, parking at a turnout about 1500 feet from the highway.

• **North Country National Scenic Trail, Jay Cooke State Park segment** – This seven-state trail enters Minnesota from Wisconsin at Jay Cooke State Park. Park in the lot for the swinging bridge and head north across Minn. Hwy. 210 to Forbay Lake for a scenic 1-mile (2-miles round trip) segment of it within the state park, via the **White Pine** and **C.C.C. trails**.

• **Organtz Trail** – The 2-mile loop in Jay Cooke State Park heads through a forest of aspen, birch and maple, which makes for a great autumn hike; along the St. Louis River are heavy deposits of red clay left here by retreating glaciers some 10,000 years ago. Park in the lot for the picnic area east of the swinging bridging.

• **Willard Munger State Trail, Carlton segment** – A large parking lot with picnic shelter is along County Road 1 (Third Street) between North and South avenues. This route heads east/north toward Duluth with a connecting trail to Jay

Cooke State Park.

• **Willard Munger State Trail, Thomson segment** –
Parking is available off the west side of County Road 210
south of Dalles Avenue and north of the trail in Thomson.
Heading west on the trail brings you past some rock
formations and to a bridge over the rapids-laden St. Louis
River.

• **Willard Munger State Trail, Alex Laveau Memorial
Trail, Carlton segment** – In Carlton, use the lot along County
Road 1 (Third Street) between North and South avenues;
walk south off the side of County Road 1, accessing the trail
after crossing Otter Creek. Head southeast through wooded
areas and rock outcroppings.

• **Willard Munger State Trail, Alex Laveau Memorial
Trail, Wrenshall segment** – On non-school days, park in the
Wrenshall Elementary School lot northeast of the building;
walk southeast on Pioneer Drive for an access road to the
trail. The southeastern route runs through a nice mix of
forest and farmland.

• **Yellow Birch Trail/Gandy Dancer State Trail, state
line segment** – The 3.2-mile round trip trail in the Nemadji
State Forest is entirely wooded. To reach the trailhead, from
north of Nickerson take County Road 146 to County Road
145 then Harlis Road/County Road 363 (which upon
entering the forest becomes Harlis Forest Road); a parking
area is located where the forest road intersects with the
Yellow Birch Trail. Take the Yellow Birch Trail for 0.3 miles
to the Gandy Dancer Trail, where there's a shelter. Go north
on the Gandy Dancer for 1.3 miles, crossing two branches of
the State Creek Trail, and turn back at the Wisconsin border.

• For more Carlton County hikes, see this title's sister
book, **Headin' to the Cabin: Day Hiking Trails of Northeast Minnesota**.

St. Louis County, Minn.

An incredible number of great hiking trails await in St. Louis County, mainly in outdoors-minded Duluth. Two major walking paths – the Superior Hiking Trail and the Willard Munger State Trail – begin in the city, with the former heading up the North Shore and the latter south toward Minneapolis-St. Paul. Two major bridges connect Superior to St. Louis County.

Park Point Nature Trail
City of Duluth

Sand dunes, a lighthouse ruin, and an old growth pine forest await day hikers on the Park Point Nature Trail in northern Minnesota.

The 4.4-miles round trip trail runs along the Minnesota portion of the world's largest freshwater sandbar. At 10 miles in length, Minnesota and Wisconsin Points form a natural harbor that makes Duluth-Superior major international ports.

To reach the trailhead from Interstate 35, in downtown Duluth take the Lake Avenue exit south. Follow the road over the Aerial Lift Bridge onto Minnesota Point. On the point, the road becomes Minnesota Avenue. After passing Park Point but before reaching Sky Harbor airport, park off the road. The trail begins where Minnesota Avenue ends.

For about 0.3 miles, the trail runs alongside a fence on the airport's north side. Lake Superior stretches beyond the beach to the north and east, but the view soon gives way to an old growth pine forest.

The white and red pines soaring into the sky over the trail are typical of evergreens that grow along sandbars and peninsulas in coastal areas. They are protected as part of the Minnesota Point Pine Forest Scientific and Natural Area.

Pumping stations for the cities of Superior and Cloquet's drinking water halve the pine forest at 0.9 miles from the trailhead.

Upon leaving the pines, the fairly flat trail goes up and down a little over grassy sand dunes. A number of spurs lead to either side of the sandbar; to the south/west is the Wisconsin mainland and city of Superior while to the north/east is Lake Superior.

You also can head over the sand dunes, but walking in soft sand often is harder than one might think. In addition, you want to stay on the trail to avoid stepping on heather and lichens that are common in what locals call "The Barrens."

If looking to dip your feet into the water, try the south/west side of the bar. The harbor water generally is warmer than that of the vast freshwater lake.

The Point Zero Lighthouse ruins are on the south/west side of the trail at 1.6 miles in. Spur trails lead to the lighthouse, which was built in 1858. A little farther along the walk are the buoy depot ruins.

At 2.2 miles, the trail reaches its end at the concrete walls for the Superior Entry. This is the channel in which ships leave or enter Lake Superior. Opposite the entry is the Wisconsin portion of the sandbar with a modern, orange-roofed and white-walled lighthouse on the breakwall.

The beach between the sentry and the Minnesota Point breakwall is a nice spot for a picnic. Known as The Cove, the water there is warmer than that elsewhere on the sandbar's lakeside beaches. Driftwood also can be collected.

After taking in the view, retrace your steps back to the parking area.

Before hitting this trail, make sure everyone in your party

can identify poison ivy. It does grow at various spots along the way but can be avoided by not bushwhacking.

• *Also see:* **Wisconsin Point Trail** in Lake Superior Country

The Lakewalk
City of Duluth

Fantastic views of Lake Superior, a historic lift bridge, and a walk on a pier await day hikers of the Duluth Lakewalk.

An urban trail, the Lakewalk runs along the Lake Superior shoreline for several miles. The route described here, about 3-miles round trip, takes walkers past several of the paved trail's major highlights.

June through August mark the best time to visit Duluth, when lakeshore temperatures provide welcome relief from inland heat waves. Sometimes remnants of piled snow remain in Duluth parking lots past Memorial Day. Still, depending on the year, late May and early September can be pleasant during the day though chilly at night.

To hike the Lakewalk, park at the Fitger's Inn ramp off East Superior Street. Through the building's backside, head to a platform for a vista of shimmering Lake Superior then take the staircase down to the Lakewalk, which serves as the urban segment of the Superior Hiking Trail. Turn right/southwest.

The first stop is a side trail that passes the Duluth Veterans Memorial. The half-dome pays homage to veterans from the city who gave their life during wars of the past century.

Beyond the memorial, the Lakewalk parallels Interstate 35 and railroad tracks and so can be a bit noisy. Lake Superior's blue waters and its light lap of the shores as gulls glide overhead will be enough to distract you, though.

At Corner-of-the-Lake Park, the Lakewalk veers away from the freeway and railroad, heading south along a beach.

In the distance is the Aerial Lift Bridge with the Wisconsin shoreline beyond.

At 1.5 miles into the hike, you'll reach Canal Park and the lift bridge. Before walking over to the bridge, turn left/ northeast onto North Pier for the Duluth Harbor North Breakwater Lighthouse (The South Breakwater Outer Lighthouse is on the pier on the other side of the Duluth Entry waterway.). After the sojourn on the pier, head back to the bridge.

A Duluth landmark, the 390-foot-long Aerial Lift Bridge was constructed in 1929. In addition to age, its vertical lift bridge design is rare. It still operates today, rising up to 30 times daily during the shipping season.

Turning back the way you came, head over to the Lake Superior Maritime Center. The center offers displays about commercial shipping and often hosts special events from spring through autumn. Boat and walking tours also are available.

If hungry or should your dawgs need a rest, consider stopping at one of the many restaurants northwest of the maritime center. Then return the way you came to Fitger's.

The Lakewalk is a dog-friendly trail with bags for cleaning up after Fido or Queenie located at most trail entrances. Benches also can be found overlooking several peaceful vistas of the lake.

Hiking the Lakewalk north

If you want to avoid Canal Park's crowds, at Fitger's instead turn left/northeast for a 2-mile round trip hike.

The trail is squished between I-35 and railroad tracks on one side and the lake on the other, so it can be bit noisy until reaching Leif Erikson Park. The park boasts a full-scale wooden replica of a Viking ship used hundreds of years ago (Note: In 2013, the ship was moved until a new shelter could be built for it.).

Near the park's north side, take the walkway over the railroad tracks north to the Rose Garden (I-35 runs in a tunnel beneath the garden), which will delight your senses. More than 3,000 rose bushes, as well as several other flowers and herbs, grow here.

After enjoying the Rose Garden, return to the main trail via the walkway and head on back to Fitger's.

Other St. Louis County Trails

• **Chester Park Trail** – The trail loops along Chester Creek, which sits in a wooded ravine. Park on the street and access the trailhead at Fourth Street and 14th Avenue East in Chester Park.

• **Congdon Park Trail** – The trail parallels Tischer Creek, as it flows toward Lake Superior. A trailhead is at St. Marie Street and Vermilion Road in Congdon Park.

• **Grassy Point Trail** – A short trail heads over wetlands and Keene Creek near its confluence with the St. Louis River. Park at the end of Leisure Street.

• **Hartley Park trails** – Several trails run through Hartley Park, with a spur of the Superior Hiking Trail leading to the top of 1300-foot Rock Knob offering lots of scenery. Other trails head past Tischer Creek and up Hunters Hill to Gaebo Point. Park in the lot at the nature center.

• **Lester/Amity MTB Trail** – The loping trail follows wooded Amity Creek and the Lester River for several miles. Park in the turnout off Seven Bridges Road immediately south of the creek; cross the bridge north to the trailhead on the road's east side.

• **Lincoln Park Trail, Miller Creek segment** – The trail winds alongside Miller Creek in the narrow but forested Lincoln Park. The route is part of the Superior Hiking Trail. Park in the Piedmont Avenue lot immediately east of North 24th Avenue; the trailhead is south of the lot on North 24th Avenue.

• **Miller Creek Interpretive Trail** – The 0.66-mile loop circles Miller Creek behind Lake Superior College with signage for 14 points of interest. The trail can be accessed from a spur on the southwest side of LSC Entrance Road, across from the West Parking Lot.

• **Mission Creek Trail segment** – A pleasant walk alongside a stream awaits day hikers on a segment of this trail in Duluth's Fond Du Lac Park. The route, measuring in at a little under 1.2 miles round trip, is a spur for the Superior Hiking Trail.

• **Muskeg Hunter Walking Trail** – The 1.5-mile route through a woods is one of many walking paths in the Canosia Wildlife Management Area north of the Duluth International Airport. Park at the trailhead off of County Road 48/Lavaque Road north of County Road 35.

• **Peace Ridge Trail** – The 3.4-mile round trip trail heads along rugged Keene Creek then climbs through a forest to fantastic views of western Duluth atop Peace Ridge. Along the way, the trail crosses the creek over a bridge built in 1914 for motor vehicles.

• **Ridge Loop Trail** – Fantastic views of Lake Superior and raptors migrating along the shoreline await day hikers of this Duluth trail. The 0.7-mile lollipop trail reaches the highest elevations in Hawk Ridge Bird Observatory, a 315-acre nature reserve. Established during the early 1970s, Hawk Ridge is now an internationally-renowned site for watching raptors with visitors from more than 40 countries.

• **Rock Pond and Hill Hiking Trail** – Several unnamed trails run through the Bagley Nature Area, which sits on the northwest corner of the University of Minnesota Duluth campus. The 0.95-mile round trip Rock Pond and Hill Hiking Trail takes you past each of the nature area's major features: Rock Pond, Rock Hill, the woodlands, and Tischer Creek

• **Superior Hiking Trail, Enger Park segment** – A segment of the North Shore trail rambles through Enger Park, crossing Coffee Creek along the way. Park in the lot along Piedmont Avenue south of North 24th Avenue, taking West Skyline Parkway northeast into Enger Park.

• **Superior Hiking Trail, Magney-Snively Park segment** – Several miles of the North Shore trail run through forested Magney-Snively Park. A parking lot is available along West Skyline Parkway south of Stewart Creek with the trail leaving from the lot's east side.

• **Western Waterfront Trail** – The lengthy 5-mile trail at Indian Point Park circles Kingsbury Creek's confluence with the St. Louis River. Park in the lot across the street from the Lake Superior Zoo.

• **Willard Munger State Trail** – The northern tip of the trail can be accessed at a number of spots. Among the most popular with parking lots are (from south to north): off 123rd Avenue West via the Superior Hiking Trail; off Riverside Drive at Grand Avenue (Minn. Hwy. 23); and marking the trail's northern terminus, off Pulaski Street east of Grand Avenue (Minn. Hwy. 23).

• For more St. Louis County hikes, see this title's sister book, **Headin' to the Cabin: Day Hiking Trails of Northeast Minnesota**.

Best Trails Lists

Which trails are the best for watching birds? To enjoy fall colors? Walking the family dog? Here are some lists of the best Douglas County trails for those and many other specific interests.

Autumn leaves
- Schoen/Louise Parks Jeep Trails
- Drummond Woods Interpretive Trail (Bayfield County)
- Trego Nature Trail (Washburn County)

Birdwatching
- Bear Beach Trail
- Brule Bog Boardwalk Trail
- Wisconsin Point Trail

Campgrounds
- Schoen and Louise Parks Jeep Trail
- Stoney Hill Nature Trail
- Thimbleberry Nature Trail

Dog-friendly
- The Lakewalk (St. Louis County)
- Trego Nature Trail (Washburn County)

Geology
- Amnicon Falls island trails
- Big Manitou Falls overlook trails
- Brule River Outlet Trail

Handicap accessible
- Brule Bog Boardwalk Trail

• Osaugie Trail

History/Archeology
• Bois Brule-St. Croix River Historic Portage Trail
• Osaugie Trail
• Wisconsin Point Trail

Lake Superior
• Bear Beach Trail
• Osaugie Trail
• Wisconsin Point Trail

Lighthouses
• Wisconsin Point Trail
• Park Point Nature Trail (St. Louis County)

Must-do's
• Amnicon Falls island trails
• Big Manitou Falls overlook trails
• Bois Brule-St. Croix River Portage Trail
• Osaugie Trail
• Stoney Hill Nature Trail

Picnicking
• Amnicon Falls island trails
• Big Manitou Falls overlook trails
• Wisconsin Point Trail

Plant communities
• Buckley Creek Barrens Trail
• Millennium Trail
• Thimbleberry Nature Trail

Sunrises
- Stoney Hill Nature Trail
- Wisconsin Point Trail

Vistas
- Namekagon Delta Trail
- Stoney Hill Nature Trail
- Wisconsin Point Trail

Waterfalls
- Amnicon Falls island trails
- Big Manitou Falls overlook trails
- Little Manitou Falls Trail

Wildflowers
- Brule Bog Boardwalk Trail
- Saunders State Trail

Wildlife
- Thimbleberry Nature Trail
- Tri-County Corridor Trail, Amnicon State Park
- East Ridge Trail (Carlton County)

Bonus Section:
Day Hiking Primer

You'll get more out of a day hike if you research it and plan ahead. It's not enough to just pull over to the side of the road and hit a trail that you've never been on and have no idea where it goes. In fact, doing so invites disaster.

Instead, you should preselect a trail (This book's trail descriptions can help you do that.). You'll also want to ensure that you have the proper clothing, equipment, navigational tools, first-aid kit, food and water. Knowing the rules of the trail and potential dangers along the way also are helpful. In this special section, we'll look at each of these topics to ensure you're fully prepared.

Selecting a Trail

For your first few hikes, stick to short, well-known trails where you're likely to encounter others. Once you get a feel for hiking, your abilities, and your interests, expand to longer and more remote trails.

Always check to see what the weather will be like on the trail you plan to hike. While an adult might be able to withstand wind and a sprinkle here or there, if you bring kids, for them it can be pure misery. Dry, pleasantly warm days with limited wind always are best when hiking with children.

Don't choose a trail that is any longer than the least fit person in your group can hike. Adults in good shape can go 8-12 miles a day; for kids, it's much less. There's no magical number.

When planning the hike, try to find a trail with a mid-point payoff – that is something you and definitely any children will find exciting about half-way through the hike. This will help keep up everyone's energy and enthusiasm during the journey.

If you have children in your hiking party, consider a couple of additional points when selecting a trail.

Until children enter their late teens, they need to stick to trails rather than going off-trail hiking, which is known as bushwhacking. Children too easily can get lost when off trail. They also can easily get scratched and cut up or stumble across poisonous plants and dangerous animals.

Generally, kids will prefer a circular route to one that requires hiking back the way you came. The return trip often feels anti-climatic, but you can overcome that by mentioning features that all of you might want to take a closer look at.

Once you select a trail, it's time to plan for your day hike. Doing so will save you a lot of grief – and potentially prevent an emergency – later on. You are, after all, entering the wilds, a place where help may not be readily available.

When planning your hike, follow these steps:

• Print a road map showing how to reach the parking lot near the trailhead. Outline the route with a transparent yellow highlighter and write out the directions.

• Print a satellite photo of the parking area and the trailhead. Mark the trailhead on the photo.

• Print a topo map of the trail. Outline the trail with the yellow highlighter. Note interesting features you want to see along the trail and the destination.

• If carrying GPS, program this information into your device.

• Make a timeline for your trip, listing: when you will leave home; when you will arrive at the trailhead; your turn back time; when you will return for home in your vehicle; and when you will arrive at your home.

• Estimate how much water and food you will need to

bring based on the amount of time you plan to spend on the trail and in your vehicle. You'll need at least two pints of water per person for every hour on the trail.

• Fill out two copies of a hiker's safety form. Leave one in your vehicle.

• Share all of this information with a responsible person remaining in civilization, leaving a hiker's safety form with them. If they do not hear from you within an hour of when you plan to leave the trail in your vehicle, they should contact authorities to report you as possibly lost.

Clothing

Footwear

If your feet hurt, the hike is over, so getting the right footwear is worth the time. Making sure the footwear fits before hitting the trail also is worth the effort. With children, if you've gone a few weeks without hiking, that's plenty of time for feet to grow, and they may have just outgrown their hiking boots. Check out everyone's footwear a few days before heading out on the hike. If it doesn't fit, replace it.

For flat, smooth, dry trails, sneakers and cross-trainers are fine, but if you really want to head onto less traveled roads or tackle areas that aren't typically dry, you'll need hiking boots. Once you start doing any rocky or steep trails – and remember that a trail you consider moderately steep needs to be only half that angle for a child to consider it extremely steep – you'll want hiking boots, which offer rugged tread perfect for handling rough trails.

Socks

Socks serve two purposes: to wick sweat away from skin and to provide cushioning. Cotton socks aren't very good for hiking, except in extremely dry environments, because they retain moisture that can result in blisters. Wool socks or liner socks work best. You'll want to look for three-season socks, also known as trekking socks. While a little thicker than summer socks, their extra cushioning generally prevents blisters. Also, make sure kids don't put on holey socks; that's just inviting blisters.

Layering

On all but the hot, dry days, when hiking you should wear multiple layers of clothing that provide various levels of protection against sweat, heat loss, wind and potentially rain. Layering works because the type of clothing you select for each stratum serves a different function, such as wicking moisture or shielding against wind. In addition, trapped air between each layer of clothing is warmed by your body heat. Layers also can be added or taken off as needed.

Generally, you need three layers. Closest to your skin is the wicking layer, which pulls perspiration away from the body and into the next layer, where it evaporates. Exertion from walking means you will sweat and generate heat, even if the weather is cold. The second layer is an insulation layer, which helps keep you warm. The last layer is a water-resistant shell that protects you from rain, wind, snow and sleet.

As the seasons and weather change, so does the type of clothing you select for each layer. The first layer ought to be a loose-fitting T-shirt in summer, but in winter and on other cold days you might opt for a long-sleeved moisture-wicking synthetic material, like polypropylene. During winter, the next layer probably also should cover the neck, which often is exposed to the elements. A turtleneck works fine, but preferably not one made of cotton. The third layer in winter, depending on the temperature, could be a wool sweater, a half-zippered long sleeved fleece jacket, or a fleece vest.

You might even add a fourth layer of a hooded parka with

pockets, made of material that can block wind and resist water. Gloves or mittens as well as a hat also are necessary on cold days.

Headgear

Half of all body heat is lost through the head, hence the hiker's adage, "If your hands are cold, wear a hat." In cool, wet weather, wearing a hat is at least good for avoiding hypothermia, a potentially deadly condition in which heat loss occurs faster than the body can generate it. Children are more susceptible to hypothermia than adults.

Especially during summer, a hat with a wide brim is useful in keeping the sun out of eyes. It's also nice should rain start to fall.

For young children, get a hat with a chin strap. They like to play with their hats, which will fly off in a wind gust if not "fastened" some way to the child.

Sunglasses

Sunglasses are an absolute must if walking through open areas exposed to the sun and in winter when you can suffer from snow blindness. Look for 100% UV-protective shades, which provide the best screen.

Equipment

A couple of principles should guide your purchases. First, the longer and more complex the hike, the more equipment you'll need. Secondly, your general goal is to go light. Since you're on a day hike, the amount of gear you'll need is a fraction of what backpackers shown in magazines and catalogues usually carry. Still, the inclination of most day hikers is to not carry enough equipment. For the lightness issue, most gear today is made with titanium and siliconized nylon, ensuring it is sturdy yet fairly light. While the following list of what you need may look long, it won't weigh much.

Backpacks

Sometimes called daypacks (for day hikes or for kids), backpacks are essential to carry all of the essentials you need – snacks, first-aid kit, extra clothing.

For day hiking, you'll want to get yourself an internal frame, in which the frame giving the backpack its shape is inside the pack's fabric so it's not exposed to nature. Such frames usually are lightweight and comfortable. External frames have the frame outside the pack, so they are exposed to the elements. They are excellent for long hikes into the backcountry when you must carry heavy loads.

As kids get older, and especially after they've been hiking for a couple of years, they'll want a "real" backpack. Unfortunately, most backpacks for kids are overbuilt and too heavy. Even light ones that safely can hold up to 50 pounds are inane for most children.

When buying a daypack for your child, look for sternum straps, which help keep the strap on the shoulders. This is vital for prepubescent children as they do not have the broad shoulders that come with adolescence, meaning packs likely will slip off and onto their arms, making them uncomfortable and difficult to carry. Don't buy a backpack that a child will "grow into." Backpacks that don't fit well simply will lead to sore shoulder and back muscles and could result in poor posture.

Also, consider purchasing a daypack with a hydration system for kids. This will help ensure they drink a lot of water. More on this later when we get to canteens.

Before hitting the trail, always check your children's backpacks to make sure that they have not overloaded them. Kids think they need more than they really do. They also tend to overestimate their own ability to carry stuff. Sibling rivalries often lead to children packing more than they should in their rucksacks, too. Don't let them overpack "to teach them a lesson," though, as it can damage bones and turn the hike into a bad experience.

A good rule of thumb is no more than 25 percent capacity. Most upper elementary school kids can carry only about 10 pounds for any short distance. Subtract the weight of the backpack, and that means only 4-5 pounds in the backpack. Overweight children will need to carry a little less than this or they'll quickly be out of breath.

Child carriers

If your child is an infant or toddler, you'll have to carry him. Until infants can hold their heads up, which usually doesn't happen until about four to six months of age, a front pack (like a Snugli or Baby Bjorn) is best. It keeps the infant close for warmth and balances out your backpack. At the same time, though, you must watch for baby overheating in a front pack, so you'll need to remove the infant from your body at rest stops.

Once children reach about 20 pounds, they typically can hold their heads up and sit on their own. At that point, you'll want a baby carrier (sometimes called a child carrier or baby backpack), which can transfer the infant's weight to your hips when you walk. You'll not only be comfortable, but your child will love it, too.

Look for a baby carrier that is sturdy yet lightweight. Your child is going to get heavier as time passes, so about the only way you can counteract this is to reduce the weight of the items you use to carry things. The carrier also should have adjustment points, as you don't want your child to outgrow the carrier too soon. A padded waist belt and padded shoulder straps are necessary for your comfort. The carrier should provide some kind of head and neck support if you're hauling an infant. It also should offer back support for children of all ages, and leg holes should be wide enough so there's no chafing. You want to be able to load your infant without help, so it should be stable enough to stand that way when you take it off the child can sit in it for a moment while you get turned around. Stay away from baby carriers with only shoulder straps as you need the waist belt to help shift the child's weight to your hips for more comfortable walking.

Fanny packs

Also known as a belt bag, a fanny pack is virtually a must for anyone with a baby carrier as you can't otherwise lug a backpack. If your significant other is with you, he or she can carry the backpack, of course. Still, the fanny pack also is a good alternative to a backpack in hot weather, as it will reduce back sweat.

If you have only one or two kids on a hike, or if they also are old enough to carry daypacks, your fanny pack need not be large. A mid-size pouch can carry at least 200 cubic inches of supplies, which is more than enough to accommodate all the materials you need. A good fanny pack also has a place to hook canteens to it.

Canteens

Canteens or plastic bottles filled with water are vital for any hike, no matter how short the trail. You'll need to have enough of them to carry about two pints of water per person for every hour of hiking.

Trekking poles

Also known as walking poles or walking sticks, trekking poles are necessary for maintaining stability on uneven or wet surfaces and to help reduce fatigue. The latter makes them useful on even surfaces. By transferring weight to the arms, a trekking pole can reduce stress on knees and lower back, allowing you to maintain a better posture and to go farther.

If an adult with a baby or toddler on your back, you'll primarily want a trekking pole to help you maintain your balance, even if on a flat surface, and to help absorb some of the impact of your step.

Graphite tips provide the best traction. A basket just above the tip is a good idea so the stick doesn't sink into mud or sand. Angled cork handles are ergonomic and help absorb sweat from your hands so they don't blister. A strap on the handle to wrap around your hand is useful so the stick doesn't slip out. Telescopic poles are a good idea as you can adjust them as needed based on the terrain you're hiking and as kids grow to accommodate their height.

The pole also needs to be sturdy enough to handle rugged terrain, as you don't want a pole that bends when you press it to the ground. Spring-loaded shock absorbers help when heading down a steep incline but aren't necessary. Indeed, for a short walk across flat terrain, the right length stick is about all you need.

Carabiners

Carabiners are metal loops, vaguely shaped like a D, with a sprung or screwed gate. You'll find that hooking a couple of them to your backpack or fanny pack useful in many ways. For example, if you need to dig through a fanny pack, you can hook the strap of your trekking pole to it. Your hat, camera straps, first-aid kit, and a number of other objects also can connect to them. Hook carabiners to your fanny pack or backpack upon purchasing them so you don't forget them when packing. Small carabiners with sprung gates are inexpensive, but they do have a limited life span of a couple of dozen hikes.

Navigational Tools
Paper maps

Paper maps may sound passé in this age of GPS, but you'll find the variety and breadth of view they offer to be useful. During the planning process, a paper map (even if viewing it online), will be far superior to a GPS device. On the hike, you'll also want a backup to GPS. Or like many casual hikers, you may not own GPS at all, which makes paper maps indispensable.

Standard road maps (which includes printed guides and handmade trail maps) show highways and locations of cities and parks. Maps included in guidebooks, printed guides handed out at parks, and those that are hand-drawn tend to be designed like road maps, and often carry the same positives and negatives.

Topographical maps give contour lines and other important details for crossing a landscape. You'll find them invaluable on a hike into the wilds. The contour lines' shape and their spacing on a topo map show the form and steepness of a hill or bluff, unlike the standard road map and most brochures and hand-drawn trail maps. You'll also know if you're in a woods, which is marked in green, or in a clearing, which is marked in white. If you get lost, figuring out where you are and how to get to where you need to be will be much easier with such information.

Satellite photos offer a view from above that is rendered exactly as it would look from an airplane. Thanks to Google and other online services, you can get fairly detailed pictures of the landscape. Such pictures are an excellent resource when researching a hiking trail. Unfortunately, those pictures don't label what a feature is or what it's called, as would a topo map. Unless there's a stream, determining if a feature is a valley bottom or a ridgeline also can be difficult. Like topo maps, satellite photos can be out of date a few years.

GPS

By using satellites, the global positioning system can find your spot on the Earth to within 10 feet. With a GPS device, you can preprogram the trailhead location and mark key turns and landmarks as well as the hike's end point. This mobile map is a powerful technological tool that almost certainly ensures you won't get lost – so long as you've correctly programmed the information. GPS also can calculate travel time and act as a compass, a barometer and altimeter, making such devices virtually obsolete on a hike.

In remote areas, however, reception is spotty at best for GPS, rendering your mobile map worthless. A GPS device also runs on batteries, and there's always a chance they will go dead. Or you may drop your device, breaking it in the process. Their screens are small, and sometimes you need a large paper map to get a good sense of the natural landmarks around you.

Compass

Like a paper map, a compass is indispensable even if you use GPS. Should your GPS no longer function, the compass then can be used to tell you which direction you're heading. A protractor compass is best for hiking. Beneath the compass needle is a transparent base with lines to help your orient yourself. The compass often serves as a magnifying glass to help you make out map details. Most protractor compasses also come with a lanyard for easy carrying.

Food and Water

Water

As water is the heaviest item you'll probably carry, there

is a temptation to not take as much as one should. Don't skimp on the amount of water you bring, though; after all, it's the one supply your body most needs. It's always better to end up having more water than you needed than returning to your vehicle dehydrated.

How much water should you take? Adults need at least a quart for every two hours hiking. Children need to drink about a quart every two hours of walking and more if the weather is hot or dry. To keep kids hydrated, have them drink at every rest stop.

Don't presume there will be water on the hiking trail. Most trails outside of urban areas lack such amenities. In addition, don't drink water from local streams, lakes, rivers or ponds. There's no way to tell if local water is safe or not. As soon as you have consumed half of your water supply, you should turn around for the vehicle.

Food

Among the many wonderful things about hiking is that snacking between meals isn't frowned upon. Unless going on an all-day hike in which you'll picnic along the way, you want to keep everyone in your hiking party fed, especially as hunger can lead to lethargic and discontented children. It'll also keep young kids from snacking on the local flora or dirt. Before hitting the trail, you'll want to re-package as much of the food as possible as products sold at grocery stores tend to come in bulky packages that take up space and add a little weight to your backpack. Place the food in re-sealable plastic bags.

Bring a variety of small snacks for rest stops. You don't want kids filling up on snacks, but you do need them to maintain their energy levels if they're walking or to ensure they don't turn fussy if riding in a baby carrier. Go for complex carbohydrates and proteins for maintaining energy.

Good options include dried fruits, jerky, nuts, peanut butter, prepared energy bars, candy bars with a high protein content (nuts, peanut butter), crackers, raisins and trail mix (called "gorp"). A number of trail mix recipes are available online; you and your children may want to try them out at home to see which ones you collectively like most.

Salty treats rehydrate better than sweet treats do. Chocolate and other sweets are fine if they're not all that's exclusively served, but remember they also tend to lead to thirst and to make sticky messes. Whichever snacks you choose, don't experiment with food on the trail. Bring what you know kids will like.

Give the first snack within a half-hour of leaving the trailhead or you risk children becoming tired and whiny from low energy levels. If kids start asking for them every few steps even after having something to eat at the last rest stop, consider timing snacks to reaching a seeable landmark, such as, "We'll get out the trail mix when we reach that bend up ahead."

Milk for infants

If you have an infant or unweaned toddler with you, milk is as necessary as water. Children who only drink breastfed milk but don't have their mother on the hike require that you have breast-pumped milk in an insulated beverage container (such as a Thermos) that can keep it cool to avoid spoiling. Know how much the child drinks and at what frequency so you can bring enough. You'll also need to carry the child's bottle and feeding nipples. Bring enough extra water in your canteen so you can wash out the bottle after each feeding. A handkerchief can be used to dry bottles between feedings.

Don't forget the baby's pacifier. Make sure it has a string and hook attached so it connects to the baby's outfit and isn't lost.

What not to bring

Avoid soda and other caffeinated beverages, alcohol, and energy pills. The caffeine will dehydrate children as well as you. Alcohol has no place on the trail; you need your full faculties when making decisions and driving home. Energy pills essentially are a stimulant and like alcohol can lead to bad calls. If you're tired, get some sleep and hit the trail another day.

First-aid Kit

After water, this is the most essential item you can carry.

A first-aid kit should include:

• Adhesive bandages of various types and sizes, especially butterfly bandages (for younger kids, make sure they're colorful kid bandages)
  • Aloe vera
  • Anesthetic (such as Benzocaine)
  • Antacid (tablets)
  • Antibacterial (aka antibiotic) ointment (such as Neosporin or Bacitracin)
  • Anti-diarrheal tablets (for adults only, as giving this to a child is controversial)
  • Anti-itch cream or calamine lotion
  • Antiseptics (such as hydrogen peroxide, iodine or Betadine, Mercuroclear, rubbing alcohol)
  • Baking soda
  • Breakable (or instant) ice packs
  • Cotton swabs
  • Disposable syringe (w/o needle)
  • Epipen (if children or adults have allergies)
  • Fingernail clippers (your multi-purpose tool might have this, and if so you can dispense with it)
  • Gauze bandage
  • Gauze compress pads (2x2 individually wrapped pad)

- Hand sanitizer (use this in place of soap)
- Liquid antihistamine (not Benadryl tablets, however, as children should take liquid not pills; be aware that liquid antihistamines may cause drowsiness)
- Medical tape
- Moisturizer containing an anti-inflammatory
- Mole skin
- Pain reliever (a.k.a. aspirin; for children's pain relief, use liquid acetaminophen such Tylenol or liquid ibuprofen; never give aspirin to a child under 12)
- Poison ivy cream (for treatment)
- Poison ivy soap
- Powdered sports drinks mix or electrolyte additives
- Sling
- Snakebite kit
- Thermometer
- Tweezers (your multi-purpose tool may have this allowing you to dispense with it)
- Water purification tablets

If infants are with you, be sure to also carry teething ointment (such as Orajel) and diaper rash treatment.

Many of the items should be taken out of their store packaging to make placement in your fanny pack or backpack easier. In addition, small amounts of some items – such as baking soda and cotton swabs – can be placed inside re-sealable plastic bags, since you won't need the whole amount purchased.

Make sure the first-aid items are in a waterproof container. A re-sealable plastic zipper bag is perfectly fine. As Douglas County sports a humid climate, be sure to replace the adhesive bandages every couple of months, as they can deteriorate in the moistness. Also, check your first-aid kit every few trips and after any hike in which you've just used it, so that you can replace used components and to make sure medicines haven't expired.

If you have older elementary-age kids and teenagers who've been trained in first aid, giving them a kit to carry as well as yourself is a good idea. Should they find themselves lost or if you cannot get to them for a few moments, the kids might need to provide very basic first aid to one another.

Hiking with Children: Attitude Adjustment

To enjoy hiking with kids, you'll first have to adopt your child's perspective. Simply put, we must learn to hike on our kids' schedules – even though they may not know that's what we're doing.

Compared to adults, kids can't walk as far, they can't walk as fast, and they will grow bored more quickly. Every step we take requires three for them. In addition, early walkers, up to two years of age, prefer to wander than to "hike." Preschool kids will start to walk the trail, but at a rate of only about a mile per hour. With stops, that can turn a three-mile hike into a four-hour journey. Kids also won't be able to hike as steep of trails as you or handle as inclement of weather as you might.

This all may sound limiting, especially to long-time backpackers used to racking up miles or bagging peaks on their hikes, but it's really not. While you may have to put off some backcountry and mountain climbing trips for a while, it also opens up to you a number of great short trails and nature hikes with spectacular sights that you may have otherwise skipped because they weren't challenging enough.

So sure, you'll have to make some compromises, but the payout is high. You're not personally on the hike to get a workout but to spend quality time with your children.

Family Dog

Dogs are part of the family, and if you have children,

they'll want to share the hiking experience with their pets. In turn, dogs will have a blast on the trail, some larger dogs can be used as Sherpas, and others will defend against threatening animals.

But there is a downside to dogs. Many will chase animals and so run the risk of getting lost or injured. Also, a doggy bag will have to be carried for dog pooh – yeah, it's natural, but also inconsiderate to leave for other hikers to smell and for their kids to step in. In addition, most dogs almost always will lose a battle against a threatening animal, so there's a price to be paid for your safety.

Many places where you'll hike solve the dilemma for you as dogs aren't allowed on their trails. Dogs are verboten on some Wisconsin State Parks trails but usually permitted on those in national forests. Always check with the park ranger before heading to the trail.

If you can bring a dog, make sure it is well behaved and friendly to others. You don't need your dog biting another hiker while unnecessarily defending its family.

Rules of the Trail

Ah, the woods or a wide open meadow, peaceful and quiet, not a single soul around for miles. Now you and your children can do whatever you want.

Not so fast. Act like wild animals on a hike, and you'll destroy the very aspects of the wilds that make them so attractive. Act like wild animals, and you're likely to end up back in civilization, specifically an emergency room. And there are other people around. Just as you would wish them to treat you courteously, so you should do the same for them. Let's cover how to act civilized in the wilds.

Minimize damage to your surroundings
When on the trail, follow the maxim of "Leave no trace."

Obviously, you shouldn't toss litter on the ground, start rockslides, or pollute water supplies. How much is damage and how much is good-natured exploring is a gray area, of course. Most serious backpackers will say you should never pick up objects, break branches, throw rocks, pick flowers, and so on – the idea is not to disturb the environment at all.

Good luck getting a four-year-old to think like that. The good news is a four-year-old won't be able to throw around many rocks or break many branches.

Still, children from their first hike into the wilderness should be taught to respect nature and to not destroy their environment. While you might overlook a preschooler hurling rocks into a puddle, they can be taught to sniff rather than pick flowers. As they grow older, you can teach them the value of leaving the rock alone. Regardless of age, don't allow children to write on boulders or carve into trees.

Many hikers split over picking berries. To strictly abide by the "minimize damage" principle, you wouldn't pick any ber-ries at all. Kids, however, are likely to find great pleasure in eating blackberries, currants and thimbleberries as am-bling down the trail. Personally, I don't see any problem enjoying a few berries if the long-term payoff is a respect and love for nature. To minimize damage, teach them to only pick berries they can reach from the trail so they don't trample plants or deplete food supplies for animals. They also should only pick what they'll eat.

Collecting is another issue. In national and most state and county parks, taking rocks, flower blossoms and even pine cones is illegal. Picking flowers moves many species, espec-ially if they are rare and native, one step closer to extinction. Archeological ruins are extremely fragile, and even touching them can damage a site.

But on many trails, especially gem trails, collecting is part of the adventure. Use common sense – if the point of the trail is to find materials to collect, such as a gem trail, take judiciously, meaning don't overcollect. Otherwise, leave what you find there.

Sometimes the trail crosses private land. If so, walking around fields, not through them, always is best or you could damage a farmer's crops.

Pack out what you pack in

Set the example as a parent: Don't litter yourself; whenever stopping, pick up whatever you've dropped; and always require kids to pick up after themselves when they litter. In the spirit of "Leave no trace," try to leave the trail cleaner than you found it, so if you come across litter that's safe to pick up, do so and bring it back to a trash bin in civilization. Given this, you may want to bring a plastic bag to carry out garbage.

Picking up litter doesn't just mean gum and candy wrappers but also some organic materials that take a long time to decompose and aren't likely to be part of the natural environment you're hiking. In particular, these include peanut shells, orange peelings, and eggshells.

Burying litter, by the way, isn't viable. Either animals or erosion soon will dig it up, leaving it scattered around the trail and woods.

Stay on the trail

Hiking off trail means potentially damaging fragile growth. Following this rule not only ensures you minimize damage but is also a matter of safety. Off trail is where kids most likely will encounter dangerous animals and poisonous plants. Not being able to see where they're stepping also increases the likelihood of falling and injuring themselves. Leaving the trail raises the chances of getting lost. Staying on the trail also means staying out of caves, mines or abandoned structures you may encounter. They are usually dangerous places.

Finally, never let children take a shortcut on a switchback trail. Besides putting them on steep ground upon which they could slip, their impatient act will cause the switchback to erode.

Trail Dangers

On Douglas County trails, two common dangers face hikers: ticks and poison ivy/sumac. Both can make miserable your time on the trail or once back home. Fortunately, both threats are easily avoidable and treatable.

Ticks

One of the greatest dangers comes from the smallest of creatures: ticks. Both the wood and the deer tick are common in Douglas County and can infect people with Lyme disease.

Ticks usually leap onto people from the top of a grass blade as you brush against it, so walking in the middle of the trail away from high plants is a good idea. Wearing a hat, a long sleeve shirt tucked into pants, and pants tucked into shoes or socks, also will keep ticks off you, though this is not foolproof as they sometimes can hook onto clothing. A tightly woven cloth provides the best protection, however. Children can pick up a tick that has hitchhiked onto the family dog, so outfit Rover and Queenie with a tick-repelling collar.

After hiking into an area where ticks live, you'll want to examine your children's bodies (as well as your own) for them. Check warm, moist areas of the skin, such as under the arms, the groin and head hair. Wearing light-colored clothing helps make the tiny tick easier to spot.

To get rid of a tick that has bitten your child, drip either disinfectant or rubbing alcohol on the bug, so it will loosen its grip. Grip the tick close to its head, slowly pulling it away from the skin. This hopefully will prevent it from releasing saliva that spreads disease. Rather than kill the tick, keep it in a plastic bag so that medical professionals can analyze it should disease symptoms appear. Next, wash the bite area with soap and water then apply antiseptic.

In the days after leaving the woods, also check for signs of disease from ticks. Look for bulls-eye rings, a sign of a Lyme disease. Other symptoms include a large red rash, joint pain, and flu-like symptoms.

If any of these symptoms appear, seek medical attention immediately. Fortunately, antibiotics exist to cure most tick-related diseases.

Poison ivy/sumac

Often the greatest danger in the wilds isn't our own clumsiness or foolhardiness but various plants we encounter. The good news is that we mostly have to force the encounter with flora. Touching the leaves of either poison ivy or poison sumac in particular results in an itchy, painful rash. Each plant's sticky resin, which causes the reaction, clings to clothing and hair, so you may not have "touched" a leaf, but once your hand runs against the resin on shirt or jeans, you'll probably get the rash.

To avoid touching these plants, you'll need to be able to identify each one. Remember the "Leaves of three, let it be" rule for poison ivy. Besides groups of three leaflets, poison ivy has shiny green leaves that are red in spring and fall. Poison sumac's leaves are not toothed as are non-poisonous sumac, and in autumn their leaves turn scarlet. Be forewarn-ed that even after leaves fall off, poison oak's stems can carry some of the itchy resin.

By staying on the trail and walking down its middle rather than the edges, you are unlikely to come into contact with this pair of irritating plants. That probably is the best preventative. Poison ivy barrier creams also can be helpful, but they only temporarily block the resin. This lulls you into a false sense of safety, and so you may not bother to watch for poison ivy.

To treat poison ivy/sumac, wash the part of the body that has touched the plant with poison ivy soap and cold water. This will erode the oily resin, so it'll be easier to rinse off. If you don't have any of this special soap, plain soap sometimes will work if used within a half-hour of touching the plant. Apply a poison ivy cream and get medical attention immediately. Wearing gloves, remove any clothing (including shoes) that has touched the plants, washing them and the worn gloves right away.

For more about these topics and many others, pick up this author's **Hikes with Tykes: A Practical Guide to Day Hiking with Kids**. You also can find tips online at the author's Day Hiking Trails blog at *hikeswithtykes.blogspot.com*. Have fun on the trail!

Index

About the Author

Rob Bignell is a long-time hiker, journalist, and author of the popular "Hikes with Tykes," "Headin' to the Cabin," and "Hittin' the Trail" guidebooks and several other titles. He and his son Kieran have been hiking together for the past eight years. Before Kieran, Rob served as an infantryman in the Army National Guard and taught middle school students in New Mexico and Wisconsin. His newspaper work has won several national and state journalism awards, from editorial writing to sports reporting. In 2001, The Prescott Journal, which he served as managing editor of, was named Wisconsin's Weekly Newspaper of the Year. Rob and Kieran live in Wisconsin.

CHECK OUT THESE OTHER HIKING BOOKS BY ROB BIGNELL

"Headin' to the Cabin" series:
◆Day Hiking Trails of Northeast Minnesota
◆Day Hiking Trails of Northwest Wisconsin

"Hikes with Tykes" series:
◆Hikes with Tykes: A Practical Guide to Day Hiking with Children
◆Hikes with Tykes: Games and Activities

"Hittin' the Trail" series:
Minnesota
◆Interstate State Park (ebook only)
Wisconsin
◆Barron County
◆Bayfield County
◆Burnett County (ebook only)
◆Crex Meadows Wildlife Area (ebook only)
◆Interstate State Park (ebook only)
◆Polk County (ebook only)
◆Sawyer County
National parks
◆Grand Canyon (ebook only)

ORDER THEM ONLINE AT:
hikeswithtykes.com/hittinthetrail_home.html

WANT MORE INFO ABOUT FAMILY DAY HIKES?

Follow this book's blog, where you'll find:

Tips on day hiking with kids

Lists of great trails to hike with children

Parents' questions about
day hiking answered

Product reviews

Games and activities for the trail

News about the book series
and author

Visit online at:
hikeswithtykes.blogspot.com

www.ingramcontent.com/pod-product-compliance
Lightning Source LLC
Chambersburg PA
CBHW050537280326
41933CB00011B/1627